The Promise and the Presence

HARRY N. HUXHOLD

THE PROMISE
AND THE PRESENCE

CONCORDIA PUBLISHING HOUSE

Saint Louis

Concordia Publishing House, St. Louis, Missouri
Concordia Publishing House Ltd., London, W. C. 1
© 1965 Concordia Publishing House
Library of Congress Catalog Card No. 65-13136
MANUFACTURED IN THE UNITED STATES OF AMERICA

TO CEIL

*who listened like Mary to these sermons
at 11:00 a. m.
and attended to Martha chores
at 12:30 p. m.*

❦ Foreword ❧

When the earliest Christians said "Scripture," they meant what we call the Old Testament. This is, of course, consistently true of the writers of the New Testament. Not more than one or two instances of the word *graphē* in the New Testament (cf. 2 Peter 3:16) can be taken to mean anything but the Old Testament Scriptures. But we often forget how true it was even after the apostolic era. For example, the most learned and brilliant scholar of the ante-Nicene church was certainly Origen. A study of his incredibly massive literary output reveals how dependent he was on the Old Testament for his theology. His propensity for allegorical and typological interpretation has sometimes obscured the true situation, but modern study of Origen has come to see him once more as a *magister sacrae paginae* and preeminently as a thinker whose thought and vocabulary were saturated with the history and the imagery of the Old Testament. Augustine, too, spent a large part of his life interpreting Old Testament Scripture, especially Genesis and Psalms. The researches of Leclercq have shown that an Old Testament book — of all things, the Song of Solomon — was commented on by medieval monastic theologians more often than any other. And, in a *bon mot* of Heinrich Bornkamm that I have cited elsewhere, if Martin Luther were a member of a modern theological faculty, he would be professor of Old Testament.

The sermons in this volume, many of which I was privileged to hear as a parishioner and colleague of the author, are a serious and successful attempt to recover some of the lost power of that tradition. When Christian theology and Christian preaching drift away from their Old Testament moorings, the results are calamitous. Much of the sentimentality that passes for piety in both the pulpit and the pew comes from a surrender of this heritage — although the relation between cause and effect here is quite subtle and elusive. "The good Lord," *der liebe Gott, le bon Dieu,* has replaced the Holy One of Israel, the Redeemer from of old. Ironically this sentimentality is frequently accompanied by the most devastating moralism and legalism, which are then called Judaizing tendencies! When the Old Testament is understood and preached as it is here, that sentimentality is replaced by Biblical realism. Similarly the Scriptures of the Old Testament are the best possible antidote to the individualism that doth so easily beset us; for they are not the story of an individual or of a group of individuals but of a people, bound together by the Exodus and the covenant, sharing a memory and a destiny. Continuity with that people, then and now, is an essential element in any renewal of the Christian church. As the ancient church learned in its battle against the heresy of Marcion, a rejection of that continuity means a mutilation of the doctrine of creation, a distortion of the Christian ethic, and a paralysis in the face of the very "Gentile world" it seeks to appease.

It is my hope and earnest prayer that these sermons will serve to stimulate a deepened and renewed attention to the message of the Hebrew Bible, "ever ancient and ever new," and thus to quicken the faith and the obedience of those who read them.

JAROSLAV PELIKAN

ᴥᔓ Contents ᔕᴥ

Contents

Introduction

In the early history of the development of the Christian liturgy three lessons were normally read. An Old Testament lesson preceded the reading of the Epistle and the holy Gospel. Unfortunately this practice has fallen into disuse in many communions. This has happened in spite of the fact that most service books retain a table of Old Testament lessons appointed for the church year. Happily the new *Lutheran Service Book and Hymnal* lists an Old Testament lesson for each Sunday, and the lessons are printed in the *Lectionary*.

Reintroducing the reading of accepted pericopes of Old Testament lessons would readily convince the preacher of the merit of testing his skill at preparing a series of sermons on them. Reluctance to do so serves to strengthen the tendency toward Marcionism, a notion not at all uncommon among our lay people. If we are to offer a corrective for this view, we can do no better than to preach the Old Testament lessons.

The following series of sermons grew out of such an experience. The texts are chosen from accepted Old Testament pericopic systems. The texts for Christmas and Easter are taken from the New Testament for the obvious reason that the New Testament event should be the basis for the celebration of these feasts. But even these texts show their relationship to the Old Testament.

The sermons are chosen for their relationship to the standard Gospel appointed for the day of the church year. The texts are expounded in the light of the Gospel for the day. The sermons are liturgical in that the preaching of the text in many instances relates itself quite readily to the sacraments of Holy Baptism and the Lord's Supper.

The sermons are for the most part expository. More time is spent in exposition because the texts are less familiar to the people than the greater share of our New Testament texts. The expositions are set down in the context of both Testaments on the assumption that the Old Testament interprets the New Testament and vice versa. The expositions are Christocentric in the conviction that "in many and various ways God spoke of old to our fathers by the prophets; but in these last days He has spoken to us by a Son." (Hebrews 1:1 RSV)

I am indebted to Marie Hinz for her painstaking efforts in typing the manuscript; to Jaroslav Pelikan, Jr., who as a pulpit associate at Palos Park, Ill., urged me to continue to preach the Old Testament; and to Rabbi Abraham J. Heschel, who in a seminar at the University of Minnesota in the spring quarter of 1960 deeply enriched the insight that "the heart of the Old Testament is not justice but love."

Minneapolis, Minnesota

HARRY N. HUXHOLD

Lift Up Your Heads

⊷ The earth is the Lord's and the fullness thereof, the world and those who dwell therein; for He has founded it upon the seas and established it upon the rivers. Who shall ascend the hill of the Lord? And who shall stand in His holy place? He who has clean hands and a pure heart, who does not lift up His soul to what is false and does not swear deceitfully. He will receive blessing from the Lord and vindication from the God of his salvation. Such is the generation of those who seek Him, who seek the face of the God of Jacob. Lift up your heads, O gates, and be lifted up, O ancient doors, that the King of Glory may come in! Who is the King of Glory? The Lord, strong and mighty, the Lord, mighty in battle! Lift up your heads, O gates, and be lifted up, O ancient doors, that the King of Glory may come in! Who is this King of Glory? The Lord of hosts, He is the King of Glory! ⊱

Psalm 24 (RSV)

⋖ Lift Up Your Heads ⋗

ONE of the many outstanding features of the Christian church year is that it does not begin with the birth of our Lord. At first glance one might reasonably expect it to do so. One could logically assert that a remembrance of the life of our blessed Lord should begin at the beginning of His record. Yet such commemoration would conceivably miss the significance and meaning of His life and His coming to us.

It is the season of Advent which serves to remind us that the coming of the King was a climax to that which God had already been doing in the past. In the history of the Children of Israel God had continuously and consistently revealed Himself to His people, both in the normal course of events and in His mighty deeds. And all these events gave promise of the great hour, the hour of the Messiah, the Messianic period, in which God through His Servant would actively participate in human history. We now identify that hour and the Messiah as the Christ's coming.

But this has meaning for us also only to the degree that we understand that the God who disclosed Himself to Israel of old and in the person of Jesus Christ still comes to us in all of history. He is no less active in the present than He was in the past. He is no less discernible than He was in the past. And He comes again always with the promise that He shall come again in glory.

It is of no small importance then that Advent should be called the preparation. For how can one give himself to the full impact of God's advent, His coming to us, unless he gives himself in prayerful meditation to all that is contained in the promise of His coming? It is to such thoughtful preparation that our psalm calls us when it cries, "Lift up your heads."

Look at Ourselves

This psalm urges us to look at ourselves.

Our psalm begins on the prelude: "The earth is the Lord's and the fullness thereof, the world and those who dwell therein; for He has founded it upon the seas and established it upon the rivers." God can lay claim to all the creation as His. He made it. He formed it. He sustains it. And all the creation and all who live therein, all the creatures of His hand are in debt to Him.

But the psalmist immediately raises the question, "Who shall ascend the hill of the Lord? And who shall stand in His holy place?" Who can come into the presence of God? Who can have relationship with Him? Who dares to presume that he can confront God? Who may stand in the brightness of His holiness?

The answer is: "He who has clean hands and a pure heart, who does not lift up his soul to what is false and does not swear deceitfully." Surely this is not one who is innocent, one who is without sin. But it is one who does not falsify himself, who does not try to deceive God. He does not falsify himself by covering for his sins or trying to deceive by covering sin with works tainted by false motives. The point is that we can approach God only as we are.

In the introduction to one of his plays Tennessee Williams tells the story of a little girl he had seen playing dress-up. Dressed up in high heels and adult dress, she had gone unnoticed. Frustrated she stomped and called out, "Look at me, look at me!" And in the midst of her temper tantrum she toppled into one heap of soiled costume. Mr. Williams' point was that much of adult behavior is nothing more than the frustrated call, "Look at me. Look at me."

The point for you and me here is that we cannot stomp before God in deceiving and make-believe costumes of behavior and shout at Him to "look at us." For then we should only snag ourselves in the dress of our deceit and the mask of our lies. Then God would neither hear us nor pay attention to us.

We must come "with clean hands and a pure heart." We can come only in the nakedness of our souls, empty of all righteousness and holiness, but honest in this one thing — that we know who we are, helpless in need of the Helper, the weak in need of Him who is our Strength, the children of death in need of Him who is the Life, the unholy in search of Him who is the Holy, the unblessed in need of His blessing.

"Such is the generation of those who seek Him, who seek the face of the God of Jacob," says the psalmist. These are they who look for the blessing to come from God, who trust that the God whom they seek is the God of salvation, who gives salvation. He is the God who vindicates, who declares righteous, who wipes away all guilt because He is the Provider of the salvation. He is the God of Jacob. That is, He is the God of a promise which He made to Jacob and to all the house of Israel. He would be their God. He would deliver them. He would be their God forever. He would not forsake them. He would tent forever with them in a kingdom that would have no end.

Such should be our hope. To look elsewhere for hope is always to return to ourselves and to discover that the more we search within ourselves the less we have to hope in, until finally we should become devoured by our hopelessness. One of the characters in T. S. Eliot's *The Cocktail Party* confesses that hell is really oneself when one is alone and there is nothing to escape from and nothing to make an escape to.

Our preparation to meet God in His hill, to ascend to His holy place, to seek the face of the God of Jacob, should save us from the frustration and loneliness of the final hell within us. It is our awareness of His personal presence in our lives that saves us from the loneliness. It is our willingness to give ourselves to Him in response to His promises to us that enables us to look away from the emptiness in us and respond to the call, "Lift up your heads."

We Look to Him

To those who would seek the face of the God of Jacob, who would press the promise which God has made, the psalmist calls out: "Lift up your heads, O gates, and be lifted up, O ancient doors, that the King of Glory may come in! Who is the King of Glory? The Lord, strong and mighty, the Lord, mighty in battle! Lift up your heads, O gates, and be lifted up, O ancient doors, that the King of Glory may come in. Who is this King of Glory? The Lord of hosts, He is the King of Glory!" This is the picture of a mighty king coming to his city. The gates of the city are to open and permit him triumphal entry.

The significance for us here is that we are that city. We are a spiritual city, God's Zion. And the spiritual doors of our hearts are to open for Him to come and dwell there. They are everlasting doors, because God has promised to come and dwell there for all eternity, and no one shall be able to separate us from Him. This King to whom we are to give admittance is the Lord strong and mighty, the Lord who came to do battle for us, who came to destroy our enemies — our fear, our anxiety, our guilt, our sin, our tempter, and even our death.

The Jews of old Jerusalem could take heart from this psalm as they heard its invitation in temple and synagog and as they repeated it in their homes. God, their God, the God of heaven and earth, came to their hearts to dwell with them. George Frederick Handel could take this psalm and use it in his great oratorio, *The Messiah*, as a triumphal announcement that the Christ had conquered sin and death so that He might ascend to the everlasting doors of heaven which should receive Him. In the oratorio this psalm is the picture of Christ's glorious ascension. And today, on this first day of Advent, the psalm comes to remind you and me that He whom the heavens cannot contain comes to make His abode with us. Therefore we are to lift up our heads and open the gates of our hearts.

What Advent is to do for us is to destroy all vague notions about God, to erase the easy illustrations of His power, to drown out the empty recitations about His person and substitute the reality of His coming to us. Advent seeks to arouse in us the awareness that God confronts us, that He stands in our lives, that He calls to us, speaks to us, and demands of us. Even as He came in the person of Jesus Christ, so He continues to come in Word and sacrament. As He called men to follow the Christ, He continues to summon us.

Advent is the great shout to look up and to behold Him. We begin timidly, ashamedly, knowing that we have no right to behold Him, to come to His holy hill, to stand in His holy place. It is a timid dare. And yet we remain on the strength of the encouragement which He Himself gave. And we receive Him.

In the school boys' story of the great ball player Lou Gehrig, *The Pride of the Yankees,* his biographer Frank Graham tells of his favorite pastime after the games at Yankee Stadium. He liked to play in the streets with the neighbor kids. In those games he wore a sweat shirt, an old pair of pants, and old baseball shoes from which he pried the spikes. Every evening after dinner he was thrilled to be out there hitting to the boys. For them Lou Gehrig was no ordinary hero, not just a name, not just a player one watched, a person one could tag after in the hopes of getting an autograph. He was one of them. He was real. He shared his life with them and they with him.

And so Advent serves to remind us that God is not an idol, a hero about whom we may speculate, but He is the God who comes to us to share His life with us.

The Messiah Is a Prophet

◄§ The Lord your God will raise up for you a Prophet like me from among you, from your brethren — Him you shall heed — just as you desired of the Lord your God at Horeb on the day of the assembly, when you said, "Let me not hear again the voice of the Lord my God or see this great fire anymore, lest I die." And the Lord said to me, "They have rightly said all that they have spoken. I will raise up for them a Prophet like you from among their brethren; and I will put My words in His mouth, and He shall speak to them all that I command Him. And whoever will not give heed to My words which He shall speak in My name, I Myself will require it of him." §►

Deuteronomy 18:15-19 (RSV)

⊷§ *The Messiah Is a Prophet* ₰⊷

WHEN our blessed Lord lived and walked among men, there were various opinions concerning His identity. That He belonged to the ranks of the rabbis, the teachers, was not disputed. But there was considerable consternation over the authority of His office and the validity of His work. Some recognized Him as something more than a teacher. They saw Him as a prophet. And in the Hebrew tradition the role of prophet was something more than the role of teacher. In fact, the Messianic hope in one form was expressed in the hope of a return of Moses.

Thus we read in the Gospel according to St. John that when our Lord performed the sign of the great feeding, the people said of Him, "This is of a truth that Prophet that should come into the world" (John 6:14). With the growth of such rumors the Lord Jesus at Caesarea Philippi found it necessary to ask His disciples, "But who do you say that I am?" (Mark 8:29). In this Advent season the question falls upon us. In order to give answer, to gain proper insights into the life of Jesus, and to evaluate properly His ministry among men we must have some understanding of the role of the prophet.

God Sends the Prophet

The prophet was regarded as one who comes with a distinct and definite word from God. The prophet is a spokesman for God. The Hebrew word for prophet means simply a spokesman. He is a speaker. We have added greatly to this meaning in the light of what we know that the prophets had to say and what their function came to be. The whole tradition of the prophets in Israel is greatly enhanced by our hindsight. But let us begin at the beginning.

The great tradition of the prophets in Israel began with the historical personage of Moses. It was Moses who felt the real presence of God in life and history. By an intense experience he felt the call of God to deliver his people from the land of bondage. And as he moved his people out of the province of the Pharaohs, he discerned the providential hand and guiding rule of God in all the little and large events that confronted his people. It was Moses who ascended Mount Sinai to mediate a covenant between God and the Children of Israel. The covenant, the Word which Moses received from God, was the Word which Moses spoke to the people. This covenant was an agreement between two unequal parties. It was like a covenant made between a conqueror and the vanquished. They had nothing to offer but obedience. In return the King offered protection. So God offered everything to this people. He was to be their God, and they were to be His people. Moses was the mediator, the go-between for God and man. He was the spokesman for God. This covenant was to be protected by moral, ceremonial, economic, and social laws. It was not as though these laws could add anything to the covenant. But all these laws were to create a climate, an atmosphere of life, in which the Children of Israel could better remember the covenant which God had made with them and their fathers Abraham, Isaac, and Jacob, that God, their God, was the God of their salvation who would establish a kingdom for everlasting.

Lest they should forget, God established among them the office of the prophet, who like Moses would bring to them the Word of God, a word from God. The passage which I read to you is a section from the description of the prophetic office. The foregoing passage is a warning against the abominations of other nations. The words following are a guide as to how the people could determine whether a prophet was sent of God or not.

There followed after Moses a succession of prophets who made known the will of God as they experienced it in the struggle of their own lives and as they saw it in the lives of God's people. But it was not simply out of the experience of their own history that they spoke. They interpreted history and social conditions in the light of God's will and His covenant. They knew themselves to be called as the very instruments of God's design in history. When they witnessed indifference to God's covenant and mockery of His holy will, they felt compelled to bring once more a word from God. Because they were possessed by the very Word, they did not fear the threat of angry kings or the terror of the mob or even excommunication from the religious community. They were lonely men, crying out against the world in the hope that they could bring God's people once more into the covenant relationship with God.

Into this succession of prophets our blessed Lord Himself stepped. He came to the holy city of Jerusalem, knowing full well that it was the Jerusalem that killed the prophets and stoned them that were sent unto it. Yet like the great prophets before Him He knew that this was His mission. He had the Word of God to deliver to His people. To them He said:

As My Father hath taught Me, I speak these things. (John 8:28)

The Father which sent Me, He gave Me a commandment what I should say and what I should speak. (John 12:49)

Whatsoever I speak therefore, even as the Father said unto Me, so I speak. (John 12:50)

It was in this proclamation of the Father's words, His commandments, and His covenant that our Lord overshadowed the prophets before Him. It is for this reason that the Christian church has interpreted this passage to be a promise of the coming of the Christ. The words "The Lord your God will raise up for you a Prophet like me from among you, from your brethren" have been taken as a reference to the Christ. No other was so likened unto Moses. Among his successors there was no peer. They only kept alive the tradition of Moses. But Christ was like Moses in that He gave a covenant to God's people. Moses brought to his people the covenant of old. Jesus gave the new covenant. Both gave revelation of God. Both were mediators.

It is this passage which makes much of the mediation of Moses. The people came and asked that he be their mediator, for they were afraid to come into the presence of God. Christ was likewise the Mediator for us, who do not dare to stand in the presence of God. By His prayer, by His life, and by His death He negotiates the eternal pact with God that we shall be everlastingly on friendly terms.

Therefore we say He is like unto Moses, but we say He is even greater than Moses. He is the final Fulfillment of the promise which God through Moses had made to His people.

God Gives His Word Through the Prophet

A second feature of the prophetic office is that the word of the prophet should be obeyed. Our text says: "Him you shall heed . . . And whoever will not give heed to My words which He shall speak in My name, I Myself will require it of him."

The word of the prophet should be obeyed because it comes from God. In this foregoing section God warns against the abomination of the nations. The distinction between the heathen and the Hebrews is that the Hebrews are to avoid the methods of divination — the enchanters, the charmers, the wizards, the necromancers, and the like. All around them the Israelites were to see peoples who would do their best to influence the spirit world, who would employ devious methods to satisfy their curiosity concerning the spirit world. To us the uniqueness of the Hebrew prophet was that he was not manipulating the spirit world by a word from man but that he was influencing man by a word straight from God. And thus as God reveals Himself fully in the Christ, He speaks to us to be heard, to be obeyed, to be accepted.

But still men will try their own word rather than trust this Word from the Prophet. In the day of the Old Testament prophets people rarely heeded them. The very people whom they were warned about influenced them greatly. In our own time we continue to be influenced by strange charmers around us. Max Rezwin in his introduction to a collection of sick jokes, grim cartoons, and bloody marys says that the person laughing at a sick joke is reflecting as much superstition as a primitive Bushman in the middle of Kalahari. In the most advanced society of the world we express our fear of death, disease, and misfortune by verbalizing the taboo with jokes and snickers.

Yet this is only one attempt among many that men employ rather than give obedience to the Word which God speaks to us through His Prophet Jesus. If, as Mr. Rezwin suggests, we can affirm life through a sick joke, what folly this is in the face of the Word which God gives us, that in the Christ there is life and salvation. Far better it would be if we were to affirm life by obedience and trust to His Word than to make the feeble attempt of hearty but sick laughter.

This we must see. The Word which our Lord commands us to obey is His own Word of glory. It is a Word of victory over death. It neither avoids hardship, heartache, pain, sorrow, or death itself, but it gives glorious victory. If it demands of us, if it commands us, if it calls us to sacrifice, if it forbids us, if it denies us, if it urges us, it does so that we might not forget the glory it holds in store for us, the glory of life in God and with God. It is a Word of glory we listen to, therefore we are warned not to live ingloriously. It is a Word of hope, therefore we are assured that we need not live as though we had no hope. It is a Word of salvation, therefore we are reminded that we can live confidently.

But this unique Word of glory to which we should listen as God speaks to us through the Christ also has something of finality about it. We must listen while we can. We should hear while we may. We should trust it now. It is either — or. Either we shall trust this Word of grace in Christ, or we shall forfeit the love of heaven. All of life is opportunity to accept God. It is either that or it is death. Our text states that God says, "Whoever will not give heed to My words . . . I Myself will require it of him." And life does not repeat itself. There is no playback. It is as Thomas Harrow says in Marquand's novel, *Women and Thomas Harrow*, that when you get a kick in the pants, if you have any sense, you know you've deserved it. Then you are apt to begin wondering what you could have done differently and you wish you could have the film played back. But you can't live life over, and don't ever try.

God, who speaks to us through His Prophet Jesus, says that there is no need to have the film of our life played back. You don't have to live life over. By the Word of the Prophet Jesus, God destroys and puts to death the old life of sins, errors, and mistakes. He slays us with this Word. This Word becomes the sword by which He puts to death the body of sin. But by the Word He also raises us to life. By the Word He absolves us and gives us life.

How this Word of God works in our lives was manifested in the life of the Prophet Jesus. Jesus lived this Word. He taught this Word. He died by this Word. He was raised by this Word. Thus He is both Prophet and Word.

Let us listen to Him!

The Advent Covenant

⋦§ Behold, the days are coming, says the Lord, when I will make a new covenant with the house of Israel and the house of Judah, not like the covenant which I made with their fathers when I took them by the hand to bring them out of the land of Egypt, My covenant which they broke, though I was their Husband, says the Lord. But this is the covenant which I will make with the house of Israel after those days, says the Lord: I will put My law within them, and I will write it upon their hearts; and I will be their God, and they shall be My people. And no longer shall each man teach his neighbor and each his brother, saying, "Know the Lord," for they shall all know Me, from the least of them to the greatest, says the Lord; for I will forgive their iniquity, and I will remember their sin no more." §⋗

Jeremiah 31:31-34 (RSV)

The Advent Covenant

EACH year commercial houses and the United States Postal Service rush us on more quickly to the celebration of the Feast of the Nativity of our Lord. One pastor said that he would just as soon relinquish the feast completely to the men of commerce and dissociate the celebration of the birth of our Lord from the worldly feast. There is much to be said for his suggestion.

However, this year, at any rate, our Christian congregations will be keeping the feast at the same time that the world may be making a mockery of it. But if we are to observe again the Lord's birth, we must be careful to note what is involved in such a celebration. In these Advent hours we seek to understand the profound significance of His entrance into our lives.

His advent, His coming, should have the profound effect upon us of alerting us to the fact that His coming changes all of life and history. By His coming we should know that man is never alone. By His coming into time He converted the temporal into the eternal. He literally brings the eternal into the temporal so that He might rescue the temporal for eternity. By His coming He incorporates the infinite into the finite that He might make us finite creatures the temples of the infinite God.

This is what we are preparing for these Advent days. Such preparation requires a careful examination of what is involved. These are the days in which we have opportunity to reconsider the renewal of the covenant between God and us — to reexamine what it is that He offers and to note carefully what is required of us.

A New Covenant

The important thing to notice about the advent covenant is that it is a new covenant. The prophet says: "Behold the days are coming, says the Lord, when I will make a new covenant with the house of Israel and the house of Judah, not like the covenant which I made with their fathers when I took them by the hand to bring them out of the land of Egypt." These words are the very epitome of the prophet's message. They are the climax of his thought as well as the thought of the entire Old Testament. The passage is quoted in full in the Epistle to the Hebrews and is considered to be the basis for the words of our Lord Himself at the institution of the Lord's Supper. These words are the hand-forged link between the old covenant and the new. They relate the one to the other.

The relationship is this: The difference between the old covenant and the new is not in essence. As a Father God had led the Children of Israel by the hand out of Egypt. This was indeed a most gracious act. It was an act of His love in history by which He declared His love for His whole people, by which He selected them. This had been a covenant of grace. He had declared to them: "I will be your God, and you will be My people." Nothing on the part of this weak, powerless, unorganized people had merited His attention or His action. He was acting toward them as a Father. In that moment of their history He gave visible evidence and a sign that He would be their King, their Ruler, their Provider, their Redeemer. That was the covenant on His part.

The covenant on their part was that they acknowledged His presence in their lives and in their community. As a people they adopted a Law which was to be to them a sign of their obedience and their faith. By this Law God would keep alive their need for His continuing and His redeeming presence among them as the people of God.

And so this people was to live by faith. But many were the times when they forgot the covenant and did not live by the covenant. Prophets came to them to remind them of the gracious promise which God had given. They called the people from their unfaithful ways. One such prophet was Hosea. He came to tell the people that God behaved toward Israel as a faithful husband who has an unfaithful wife. In long-suffering, in patience, and in grace and forgiveness He takes back to Himself this unfaithful wife who went awhoring after other gods, who lived with other gods and gave her love to them. As God acted in love toward His erring wife, the Children of Israel, He did so on the basis of the covenant, His pledge to be a faithful God and a husband to His beloved.

This does not differ from the new covenant, in which God pledges anew His willingness to be our God, to be our forgiving Father, to be the forgiving Husband of the bride, the church. It is of some great importance to note that our blessed Lord uses the illustration of the Father and the Bridegoom to portray the love of God for His holy church.

What is different about the new covenant from the old covenant is the sign by which the covenant is manifested.

In the old covenant God manifested His love, the pledge of His faithfulness, through His acts in history. The one single act which above all else was an indication of His grace was the exodus. The people of Israel were to relive this act yearly in a great feast to impress on their children that God had intervened in their history with His grace. This single incident was the first in the series of many great acts which God had performed out of His mercy and grace.

In the new covenant God would not be confined to a people. The prophet says: "I will put My Law within them, and I will write it upon their hearts; and I will be their God, and they shall be My people. And no longer shall each man teach his neighbor and each his brother, saying, 'Know the Lord,' for they shall all know Me, from the least of them to the greatest." The same grace will be made known — they shall be My people, and I will be their God — but all will know Him. This will be obvious to men as individuals, not as a people. The prophet is emphasizing a more personal kind of faith than the cultic religion that had become a dead thing among the people. God's love will be manifest in such a way that His children will know personally that God is a gracious God.

The covenant is not bound up with tribal customs and tribal history. What God has revealed in Jesus Christ is a disclosure which all men can accept. This disclosure which God made is that He came into history to fight the burdens of man as he is locked under the burdens of his guilt, his shame, and his death. Jesus took this all upon Himself to give evidence to man that God out of His grace was willing to take the burden of man's sin upon Himself and by His grace to set his sin aside, to secure for man a place in eternity. Thus it is that the covenant is the same.

But now it is fulfilled in such a way that the final acts which God performed in Jesus Christ are the very fulfillment of the covenant. This covenant is applicable to all men everywhere. God has acted in Jesus Christ not only for a people, a tribe waiting for deliverance, but for each man as he waits to be saved from his bondage to death.

The Covenant Binds Both Parties

However, joyful as this news concerning the Advent covenant is, we must not lose sight of the fact that the covenant entered into is binding on both parties. "I shall be your God, and you shall be My people," God said to the people of ancient Israel. To be the people of God meant to accept the gracious rule of God. It is to acknowledge God as the Father, to acknowledge Him as the Bridegroom of the church.

Israel had broken the covenant. Jeremiah's long and mournful complaint was that Israel had made the covenant of none effect. She had ignored it. She had ignored it in her political, her economic, and her religious life. She had turned a deaf ear to the prophetic word about God's love and His zeal to be the Father of this people. She had believed most foolishly that her hopes rested in her own efforts to be a strong and independent people, free to make the alliances she wished, free to choose to do what she would. The freedom of her action was what she deemed was her pride as the people of God, while she ignored God.

When Israel broke the covenant, she broke her relationship with God. As Jeremiah predicted, Nebuchadnezzar took this people into captivity. In captivity Israel compounded her sin when she devised a closed system of theology which led to later exclusiveness, pride, and legalism. In all of these Israel took it upon herself to work out her own salvation instead of receiving and accepting the salvation which God by His grace gives.

Thus Israel did not recognize the declaration of the new covenant when it was given in Jesus Christ. Rather it received His declaration of God's grace in the same manner in which it received the message of Jeremiah. As Jeremiah was a prophet without honor, who was persecuted, tormented, and finally dragged away, so the Lord Jesus was persecuted and tormented until He finally died that terrible death of the cross. But God raised Him from the dead to proclaim that He is still faithful to the covenant which He has made.

It remains for us to accept the covenant of God as a testament which has been completely fulfilled so that we might be the inheritance with the Lord Jesus Christ of the eternal kingdom of God.

But this we must know these Advent days. If we are to enter into this covenant with our God, if we are to be His people, then by faith we must accept the fact that the salvation which He has given freely and fully is the only salvation. We cannot prove our unfaithfulness or our unfaith by trying to make out our own answers to the problems of our own guilt and death. Rather we are to give ourselves completely to Him by faith. We trust that when we do sin, He, and He only, will grant the forgiveness of our sins. For this, says Jeremiah, is the sign of the new covenant: "I will forgive their iniquity, and I will remember their sin no more." This is the test of the new covenant. When we readily confess our sins and readily receive the forgiveness which He gives, then we keep our side of the covenant.

What a bargain this God makes with us! He gives us all things, gives us our salvation, daily grants us forgiveness.

And our end of the bargain is that we should daily accept His goodness. In Christ Jesus He has made it as plain as He can that He desires to be our God. In the cross and empty tomb we have the pledges of the covenant. Our pledge to Him is our trust and faith that Jesus is both Christ and Lord. In Christ He is our God, and in Christ we become His people.

The Advent Judgment

❧ *For behold, the day comes, burning like an oven, when all the arrogant and all evildoers will be stubble; the day that comes shall burn them up, says the Lord of hosts, so that it will leave them neither root nor branch. But for you who fear My name the Sun of Righteousness shall rise with healing in Its wings. You shall go forth leaping like calves from the stall. And you shall tread down the wicked, for they will be ashes under the soles of your feet on the day when I act, says the Lord of hosts.* ❧

Malachi 4:1-3 (RSV)

৵৩ The Advent Judgment ৪৵

FOR many, Christmas will bring the pain that it brought to little Bobby Cox in *Merry Christmas, Mr. Baxter*. Bobby was Mr. Baxter's grandson. Mr. Baxter took Bobby on a tour of the department store on Bobby's Christmas vacation. The excursion included four hamburgers, a black-and-white soda, and a tummyache that canceled out all the pleasure of the afternoon.

If Bobby had been a wee bit wise at all, he should have known that the real fun at Schwarz's toy store should have been to be with Grandpa and let him suggest some choices for consumption.

And so, too, if we should like to save ourselves the pains that follow our prodigious appetites for foolish things, it would be good for us to know that the real joy in God's world is to be with Him and to know that He comes to us to bring us the great gift of His love.

His coming then could pose a judgment for us — a judgment that is profound and eternal. If on the one hand we discern that in His presence there is joy and pleasure forevermore, very well. But if we fail to recognize this, then we create for ourselves a terror and burden that would force us to conclude that it would have been far better that we had never known His name or heard of His Christmas.

The prophet who writes in the Book of Malachi has something to say about the judgment that takes place at His coming.

The Old Era Is Under Judgment

The prophet says that when Christ comes, the day of the Messiah will be "burning like an oven, when all the arrogant and all evildoers will be stubble; the day that comes shall burn them up, says the Lord of hosts, so that it will leave them neither root nor branch."

The prophet was describing for the people the effects of the Messianic age on those that did not fear the name of the Lord and did not accept His covenant promises. It was important for him to do this, because the people to whom he addressed himself were becoming impatient with nothing but promises. These were the people of the reconstruction days after the Babylonian Exile. They had returned to their land with hope burning in their hearts that they would be able to rebuild their country and recapture their former glory. Years had passed. Their lot was anything but a glorious one. They were harassed on all sides, and their city was still not rebuilt. In the midst of their suffering they wanted to know why their suffering was prolonged.

The prophet gave answer. First, a good deal of suffering is self-imposed. When men fail in their obligations to God and their neighbor, they may expect retribution for their sins of omission. When they commit crimes against God and their neighbor, they may expect judgment for their sins of selfishness or hostility. And the prophet saw the evidence of this in the life of this people. The index of their faithlessness to God was their worship. They were giving poor sacrifices, not giving their full tithes, and in general displaying a halfhearted interest in the faith. That was one answer. So if one was worried about suffering, he should first examine himself to see if he had not created his own suffering.

The prophet also indicated, however, that not all the suffering was to be found in Judaism. The Edomites, who were also a Semitic people, had found great delight and joy in the captivity of the Jews. When the Jews returned, the Edomites continued to harass the Jews. However, now the prophet points out they had come to their own destruction. This is for the prophet an example of how justice, the justice of God, reigns among men. The Law of God does operate in history. And no nation can defy this Law without bringing doom to its own borders. As it was with Edom, so it was with Nazi Germany in our own day.

And now the third way in which God operates is the way of the Messianic day. This is the subject of our text. In the Day of the Lord, with His coming, all the arrogant and the evildoers will be consumed. His day shall burn them up. It will leave them neither root nor branch. The arrogant and the evildoers may appear to have their day, but Christ's advent will consume them.

Christ came to save. It is His mission to be the Savior of mankind, but when men refuse Him, when they turn down the offer of His grace, His coming becomes their judgment. In Christ God holds out His last offer of hope to man, but when the offer is refused, then men become as people without hope. They are left to their own destruction. What is meant to be a Word of grace for them is turned into their death warrant. What is set out for the warming of men's hearts becomes a consuming fire. The Messiah, who is sent for redemption, will linger as their Judge.

It is somewhat striking to note that the name of Christ will be plastered to mountains of parcel-post packages, sung over the loudspeakers of shopping centers throughout the length and breadth of the land, piped over radio and television stations up and down the country, splashed over every newspaper and magazine in the nation. But woe be to people who have made commerce of this name, have feasted on it, have tipped their glasses over it, and have not bothered to learn its meaning for them! For that name should mean to them that this is the day of the Lord. And if they have not lived their lives as in His day, they shall be consumed. This consuming is a progressive action, in which they will consume their lives until they are finally nothing but the stubble. They shall have neither root nor branch. Death will utterly destroy them. They may be placed in ever so beautiful a sarcophagus, but they shall be like the stubble in the earth, they shall be nothing but remains.

This is the prophet's answer. For the people who endeavor to know whether it is worthwhile to try and manage life under the covenant of God, the answer is yes. For with the advent of the Lord, in His day, justice is established. The whole secular world comes under the judgment of God. What appears to be successful outside the covenant is not successful in the eyes of God and will ultimately fail as the stubble that is without root and branch.

A New Era Dawns

But that is only a partial answer. The glory is for those who live under the covenant in the day of the Lord. For His coming is like the rising of the sun. "But for you who fear My name the Sun of Righteousness shall rise with healing in Its wings. You shall go forth leaping like calves from the stall."

To those who fear His name, who live in trust of the covenant relationship, God will burst upon them with right-eousness like the breaking forth of the glorious sun. This is a righteousness which God permits to settle on His wounded, distressed, sinful creatures. And this Sun of Righteousness is a healing for them. It is the cure for the ailments of their guilt. By this Sun, the Lord Jesus, they are made whole.

A sign of their healing, of having been made whole, will be that they will go forth like calves leaping from the stall. Their joy will be as obvious as the joy of the exhuberant calf that dances in the sun for the freedom it feels when released from the pen. So it will be for those who have ex-perienced the healing powers of God's grace. They will be freed from their guilt, from the fear of judgment, from the fear of death, to burst forth into life with all the joy and confidence of knowing that they are God's.

This is what Christ's coming into the flesh at Christmas should signify to us. God has ushered in the new day for us. Each day is always for us the dawning of the new era, when God sets aside all threats to our peace and joy.

Christ becomes the assurance that there is no reason, absolutely no reason why we should doubt God's intentions for us. Do we sometimes wonder why our neighbors are prosperous, apparently happy or contented when they have no concern for God's Word or His holy sacraments? No doubt we do. And often is the day when we are quite sure that no justice is in the world for those that love God. Then reconsider. Christ has come and is coming again. He is the Sign to behold. Not your neighbor. Your neighbor will someday perish as the stubble. But Christ is risen. He rose from His grave to demonstrate that His root and His branch was still in the Father. He is the pledge to us that the Sun of Righteousness shines on us and that we have root and branch in our God and that we shall not perish in the grave.

The police bureau reports that shoplifting is at its seasonal high just before Christmas because people despair of having gifts for their families. What a paradox! God offers His greatest Gift, Himself, and people are driven to steal a little happiness because they feel cheated unless they have what their neighbors have.

Christ's advent should mean for you and me that we have what our neighbors can never have unless they, too, see that the Sun of Righteousness has also dawned for them.

God Speaks to Us by a Son

In many and various ways God spoke of old to our fathers by the prophets; but in these last days He has spoken to us by a Son, whom He appointed the Heir of all things, through whom also He created the world. He reflects the glory of God and bears the very stamp of His nature, upholding the universe by His word of power. When He had made purification for sins, He sat down at the right hand of the Majesty on high, having become as much superior to angels as the name He has obtained is more excellent than theirs.

Hebrews 1:1-4 (RSV)

✥ *God Speaks to Us by a Son* ✥

ONE translator of the New Testament, J. B. Phillips, has reminded us that there is no mention of the celebration of the birthday of Jesus by the early church in the New Testament. It is not as though the church were against celebrations, for celebrate she did. Each week she met to celebrate with great rejoicing the event which was so excitingly alive in her memory — the resurrection. This was to her the Lord's day.

In time, however, whether early or late (we cannot be sure), the church recalled with great joy the entrance into life of Him whom she called the Lord, her Christ.

However, at all times, whether with deliberation or not, the church knew that the One who had come was God's Christ. This was important to her. It was by the special gift of the Holy Spirit that the community of believers were those who recognized that it was completely and within the character of God to send this special Person to deliver His children from their bondage to death.

Thus we have in our possession today this ancient letter to the Hebrews, which addresses us on this matter. This letter was most likely addressed to Jewish Christians in either Palestine or Rome. We may hazard the guess that its audience was the Jewish Christians in Rome. They had believed like all the young church that the return of Christ in glory was imminent. With the passing of years and no return of the Christ, their faith may have wavered, especially in the midst of persecutions. To encourage their faith and their faithfulness the writer sends them his excellent epistle.

This letter demonstrates that the Christian faith fulfills and completes the whole Jewish tradition that went before it. It does so because of the superiority, the excellency, and the divinity of the Christ. So outstanding is His character that there is a finality, a once-for-all quality that the world had not known before or since. For this reason the church could take heart and face the rigorous and consuming realities of life.

The church could take heart, for the Father had sent His Son with blessing.

The Son Has Power

For one thing, the church could take heart from this, that the Father had sent His Son with the power over all things. The writer says: "In many and various ways God spoke of old to our fathers by the prophets; but in these last days He has spoken to us by a Son, whom He appointed the Heir of all things, through whom also He created the world." This is no ordinary Son. This is He to whom God committed the power over all the heaven and the earth. This is He of whom John says that He was the Word, who existed from all eternity, the Word by whom the world was made. This personal Word is the very God, who created, rules, directs, sustains, comforts, judges, and saves the world.

God had spoken in many and various ways. In Adventtide

we remember how God had revealed Himself through the prophets and in the history of His people Israel. God had made known His will and His ways. However, the writer is indicating to us that this was neither final nor complete. Now God's speaking to us is complete, for He has spoken to us by His Son, the same Son who is Heir over all things and through whom He created the world.

Luther comments on this parallel thought in the Gospel of John: "The Word was made flesh." He says that before the moment when the Word was become flesh it was as if God were "talking to Himself." Then He speaks out loudly and expresses Himself clearly in the Word, the Christ. If we are satisfied with this analogy, then we may say that God's revelations to His people under the old covenant were the mumblings which God made to His people. But now we may say that God has spoken to us distinctly and clearly and with finality through His Son Jesus.

This Son does not reveal His Father only in what He has to say but by the authority, power, regency with which He says it. He comes as the Heir of the Father. As this Christ comes into history, He becomes the Master of history. As He comes to the creation, He is the Lord of the creation. As He comes to life, He is the Fulfillment of life. As He comes to face the forces of evil, He is the Conqueror of evil. As He comes to death, He is the Destroyer of death.

It is this that God would say to us this Christmas Day. He has sent His Son to us with the power over all things. He sends Him with the assurance that the world is not at loose ends. He still holds control. No matter how dark, how cloudy, how stormy life and history may appear, we may be assured and know with great certainty that the Christ who is over all things will give direction to our lives.

Bach in his glorious Christmas Cantata, *Ich freue mich in dir,* has the tenor render in a recitative:

An Adam may, full of fears, from God's countenance
In Paradise conceal himself!

The all-highest God gives Himself over to us: and so my heart does not take fright;

It is aware of His compassionate disposition. Out of His immeasurable goodness He has become a little child and is called my little Jesus.

What we discover anew today is that we are not alone. God has taken His place beside us. We are able to look up from our tears, our burdens, our griefs, and our sorrows to discover that God is with us. As a little child, a little Jesus, our little Brother, He comes to face it all with us, but with it He brings the power to overcome it all.

The Son Comes with Righteousness

However, God sent His Son not only with the blessing of power over all things but also with the full measure of His righteousness. The writer says: "He reflects the glory of God and bears the very stamp of His nature."

Jesus reflects the brightness of the majesty of God but not simply in the sense that He reflects it as the moon reflects the brightness of the sun. He reflects this brightness because He contains, holds, and possesses the very righteousness of God. For, the writer goes on, this Son "bears the very stamp of His nature." This stamp of His nature is the rendering of a word that originally meant an instrument which was a tool in engraving or carving. Later the tool was used for the mark stamped on an instrument. Thus the word came to mean the exact impression of an image, the marked likeness and precise reproduction. Christ brings to this world once more the very righteousness of God, the image of His holiness. Once more the creature may boast the righteousness of God. This was the same gift which God had given to the first Adam but which was lost to him when in his unfaith he decided he was not "as the gods."

Christ is God's holiness for which men seek. This is the holiness so absent in the lives of men. This is the holiness pure and unalloyed, not made artificially by pretense. This is the holiness that saves. For want of this holiness we die. For want of this holiness we live in guilt and in our shame. For want of this holiness we live ashamed in the face of one another.

This is the holiness by which "He made purification for sins." He purified us. By His life and sacrificial death He made a cleansing for us. The word used here is the word for the ceremonial washing and cleansing which the Jews made before eating. This Christ has done for us. We are clean in the sight of God. Through Christ God has declared us holy. Therefore we may employ the Christmas refrain of the angels in the great hymn of the church in her worship:

Glory be to God on high and on earth peace, goodwill toward men. We praise Thee, we bless Thee, we worship Thee, we glorify Thee, we give thanks to Thee for Thy great glory, O Lord God, heavenly King, God the Father Almighty. O Lord, the only-begotten Son, Jesus Christ, O Lord God, Lamb of God, Son of the Father, that takest away the sin of the world, have mercy upon us. Thou that takest away the sin of the world, receive our prayer. Thou that sittest at the right hand of God the Father, have mercy upon us. For Thou only art holy; Thou only art the Lord; Thou only, O Christ, with the Holy Ghost, art most high in the glory of God the Father. Amen.

The church celebrates Christmas each time she chants

this great hymn. But she does so in no hollow, sentimental way. The Christ Child comes as the Lamb, God's own sacrificial offering for our sin. Therefore the Christmas song of the church is also a prayer that in Christ God might be merciful to us.

In the Lamb of God, God has taken His place beside us. We are able to look up from the guilt and shame that fills our lives. We look up from the terror that our guilt causes us. We look up from our hiding place from God's presence. We look up from the mess of it all to find God beside us with His great gift of holiness.

The Son Comes with Victory

The third blessing with which God sends His Son is the great blessing of victory. The text reads: "When He had made purification for sins, He sat down at the right hand of the Majesty on high." The passages that follow are all spun by the writer to show the superior position, the superior victory of the Lord, the Christ.

We know this victory in our lives when we entrust our lives to the hands of the Christ. It is for us to know that this victory which the Lord Jesus won for us gives meaning and purpose to our existence, to our history. Suddenly by the power of this Christ we are transformed from the puppets of death into the living children of eternity. Swiftly by the power of this Christ we are raised from the doom into salvation.

In *Doctor Zhivago* Nikolai Nikolaievich says to his unbelieving friend, "Man does not live in a state of nature but in history, and that history as we know it began with Christ, and that Christ's Gospel is its foundation. . . . It was not until after the coming of Christ that man and time could breathe freely. It was not until after Him that men could begin to live for the future. Man does not die in a ditch like a dog — but at home, in history, while the work toward the conquest of death is in full swing; he dies sharing in this work." *

Thus it is we find our victory in the Christ. Christ becomes our future, our hope, our eternity. We are not straitjacketed by nature. We are not confined to a world of doom and death. We are not imprisoned in a hell pit of man's failure. We are not given to a pessimism about what God shall do with man. He has already given to man a new hope. By entering into our history He has redeemed history. He has intervened in the history of man's sin, of lost and hopeless causes, of inhumanity and perversity. We need no longer be threatened by what we are. He gives us the hope of renewal in His resurrection. In the resurrection we find new life. He is the Spring from whence the waters of new life flow.

Therefore we are able to add to the bursts of our Christmas hymnody this day the jubilation of Christian Keimann:

> Oh, rejoice, ye Christians, loudly,
>   For our joy hath now begun;
> Wondrous things our God hath done.
>   Tell abroad His goodness proudly
> Who our race hath honored thus
>   That He deigns to dwell with us.
> Joy, O joy, beyond all gladness,
>   Christ hath done away with sadness!
> Hence, all sorrow and repining,
>   For the Sun of Grace is shining!

* Boris Pasternak, *Doctor Zhivago*, trans. Max Hayward and Manya Harari (New York: Pantheon Books, Inc., 1958), p. 10.

We are able to look up from the terror of our future and our death to find God standing there giving His best gift to us, the gift of His holiness and His victory in our little Brother Jesus.

The Redeemer from of Old

⊰§ I will recount the steadfast love of the Lord, the praises of the Lord, according to all that the Lord has granted us, and the great goodness to the house of Israel which He has granted them according to His mercy, according to the abundance of His steadfast love. For He said, Surely they are My people, sons who will not deal falsely; and He became their Savior. In all their affliction He was afflicted, and the angel of His presence saved them; in His love and in His pity He redeemed them; He lifted them up and carried them all the days of old. But they rebelled and grieved His Holy Spirit; therefore He turned to be their enemy and Himself fought against them. Then He remembered the days of old, of Moses, His servant. Where is He who brought up out of the sea the shepherds of His flock? Where is He who put in the midst of them His Holy Spirit, who caused His glorious arm to go at the right hand of Moses, who divided the waters before them to make for Himself an everlasting name, who led them through the depths? Like a horse in the desert, they did not stumble. Like cattle that go down into the valley, the Spirit of the Lord gave them rest. So Thou didst lead Thy people to make for Thyself a glorious name. Look down from heaven and see from Thy holy and glorious habitation. Where are Thy zeal and Thy might? The yearning of Thy heart and Thy compassion are withheld from me. For Thou art our Father, though Abraham does not know us and Israel does not acknowledge us; Thou, O Lord, art our Father, our Redeemer; from of old is Thy name. ⊱

Isaiah 63:7-16 (RSV)

⋖§ *The Redeemer from of Old* §⋗

ONE of the chief problems we have in trying to look at the past is to keep a proper perspective of history. In looking back on a particular movement we are apt to jam together in our thinking incidents that were greatly separated by time. In doing just this we often lose the importance of the frame of mind of people who were a part of a movement or period of history. They lived in history as they felt they should. We need to remember this as we think about the history of Israel and the New Testament church. We are quite apt to think about the Old Testament stories as being quite different from the New Testament stories. We may be quite judgmental of the people of the day of our Lord who refused to accept the revelation which God gave of Himself in Christ Jesus, yet we may be quite sympathetic with the people of the Old Testament era because they did not see the Christ and became indifferent to the old covenant. And what we fail to understand then is that God consistently and carefully manifested Himself to His people as a gracious God. If we fail to understand this, we lose sight of the significance of the Old Testament stories. These stories are a call to faith in a redeeming God.

In the holy Gospel for today we have a good example of this problem. When Mary and Joseph bring Jesus to the temple for the rite of the presentation, two elderly people are present. There are Anna the prophetess and Simeon, of whom it is said: "He waited for the Consolation of Israel." These lovely characters are representatives not of the new testament but of the old covenant. They were believers in God's grace. What they had to say that day was based on what had been revealed to them in the past. They had heard and read such passages from the prophets which witness that God is the Redeemer from of old.

The Redeemer Is Consistent

What the prophet pours into this description of God as Redeemer from of old is, first, that He is the consistent Benefactor of His people. He says: "I will recount the steadfast love of the Lord, the praises of the Lord, according to all that the Lord has granted us, and the great goodness to the house of Israel which He has granted them according to His mercy, according to the abundance of His steadfast love. For He said, Surely they are My people, sons who will not deal falsely."

What is significant about this remembrance of God's benefactions is that God chose this people from the start. He chose Israel as His people. He made them His. He bestowed His mercies, His gifts, His goodness upon this people to elicit from them their confidence and trust. He dealt with them in a manner to make them assured that they were His sons. In response they would not be expected to deal falsely with God.

God's choice of Israel was not because of their power but because of their weakness. God did not desire to make them a weak people, but in their weakness and their dependence they permitted Him to be their God. In Egypt they needed God to be their Deliverer. In the wilderness they needed God to be their Provider. In the Promised Land they needed God to be their Defender. God came to them in their weakness and was a Father and Benefactor to them.

What this means to us is that pride stands in the way of God's operation. Man's independence is a threat to His rule. The great and beneficent God must condescend to the lowly and weak. As we seek to make Him our God, we must so understand Him. We would be His people. We would have Him choose us. We would be His sons. This means we must uproot the pride and independence from Him that will not permit relationship with Him. We must live in thankfulness for all the blessings of the steadfast love He has bestowed upon us.

The Redeemer Is Burden Bearer

The prophet also sees God as Redeemer from of old. "He became their Savior. In all their affliction He was afflicted, and the angel of His presence saved them; in His love and in His pity He redeemed them; He lifted them up and carried them all the days of old." The prophet enunciates the profound thought that God identifies with the affliction of His people. He is empathetic. He feels the hurt and the pain of His people. He knows their misery and their work.

We see how God identified with our situation in the Lord Jesus Christ. At the cross this identity with our death comes to its climax in the death of our Lord. In the resurrection He is heralded as our Savior. So God has dealt with His people from of old. God was in the history of Israel, bearing their burdens. "The angel of His presence saved them." What He did for this people was always a sign of the ultimate redemption which He gave His people.

We have this comfort, that God does not forsake us in our afflictions. The angel of His presence still saves us. He is still present with us in His Word and in His sacraments. He comes to bear our burdens, to heal our wounds, and to restore us to His righteousness. By His gracious promises and His attendant mercy He lifts us up and carries us as of old.

The Redeemer Is Leader

In the second stanza of this lesson the prophet portrays God as both an Enemy and a Leader. God desired to have this people experience His full mercy, "but they rebelled and grieved His Holy Spirit; therefore He turned to be their enemy and Himself fought against them." Not to have God as your Leader, the prophet implies, is to have Him as your Enemy. If you do not follow Him, you fight against Him. You are in opposite camps.

This was Israel's experience. God had dwelt in her camp. God had been her Leader through His servants such as Moses. He had led this people as a shepherd leads his flock. He led them through the deep. He had given them rest. But Israel rebelled against this leadership. She declared war on God by her surrender to her own pride. She made God her Enemy through her unfaith. The nations round about her became the servants of God. God permitted these nations to destroy her that she might be brought low and that in her humbled state she might call for Him to be her Leader once more.

We are confronted with this observation of the prophet. We can make God our Enemy, or we can trust Him to be our great Leader who does all things for us. We can resist His promises, fight against His will and His purpose. In that event God cannot be our Leader. He must abandon us to our unholy alliances, which eventually are our ruination. Our dependence on the creation fails us. Ultimately we die and return to the earth, forsaken and doomed to nothingness. When by faith we trust that God is our Leader, then He can lead us. He leads us by His grace. He tabernacles in our camp. He leads us against our most bitter foe. In death He is at our side. He does not abandon us. But He conquers death and gives us the victory.

The Redeemer Is Father

In the last stanza of our passage the prophet declares that God is our Redeemer from of old because He is our Father. The prophet is confident that He will not abandon His role as Father. In sure hope He invites God to have pity upon His children. "Look down from heaven and see from Thy holy and glorious habitation. Where are Thy zeal and Thy might? The yearning of Thy heart and Thy compassion are withheld from me. For Thou art our Father." God has shown forth His mercy as a Father in the past. The prophet appeals to God to help now as Father. In the midst of the trials and tumult that have come to His people He asks that the Father display His compassion upon His sons by using His zeal and His might to restore them once more.

There is no other to help. "Abraham does not know us, and Israel does not acknowledge us." Abraham and Jacob are dead. They cannot help. They were only earthly fathers. They were the progenitors of this people. But God alone is the true Father. Earthly fathers may not always be faithful. Earthly fathers die. Earthly fathers have need of a true Father also. Man's origin is really in the true Father. His life is in Him. His hope is with Him. Therefore the prophet throws Himself in faith and trust into the Father's hands. For "Thou, O Lord, art our Father, our Redeemer; from of old is Thy name."

Thus it was that Anna the prophetess and the aging Simeon by faith identified the Redeemer in the Christ. The prophet had known the history of his people well. It had been the history of God's gracious acts as Father and Redeemer from the beginning. The Christ whom Mary held was the Fulfillment of God's redeeming activity. So we today receive this Christ in the sacrament as God's assurance of His fatherly goodness and compassion for us. As we receive the Christ, we may do so in bold and daring faith. We may be assured that we can return to Him again and again in the hours of our desolation to implore His compassion, for "Thou, O Lord, art our Father, our Redeemer; from of old is Thy name."

⊸§ Remember also your Creator in the days of your youth, before the evil days come and the years draw nigh when you will say, "I have no pleasure in them"; before the sun and the light and the moon and the stars are darkened and the clouds return after the rain; in the day when the keepers of the house tremble, and the strong men are bent, and the grinders cease because they are few, and those that look through the windows are dimmed, and the doors on the street are shut; when the sound of the grinding is low, and one rises up at the voice of a bird, and all the daughters of song are brought low; they are afraid also of what is high, and terrors are in the way; the almond tree blossoms, the grasshopper drags itself along, and desire fails; because man goes to his eternal home, and the mourners go about the streets; before the silver cord is snapped, or the golden bowl is broken, or the pitcher is broken at the fountain, or the wheel broken at the cistern, and the dust returns to the earth as it was, and the spirit returns to God who gave it. §⊷

Ecclesiastes 12:1-7

⮡ Remember Your Creator in the Days ⮠ of Your Youth

THE Epiphany season reveals the Child of Bethlehem to us as the Christ, the Son of God. In the holy Gospel He is pictured as the young Lad of twelve who has entered upon His life of the church as a Son of the Command. This was a great moment for Him in His life. It was the church's first recognition of Him as one qualified to study and discuss the Word of God. And as the story reveals, it was His first declaration of how intent He was about doing just that.

In the Old Testament lesson the writer says: "Remember also your Creator in the days of your youth." This is what Jesus did. It was as if He were speaking to us from the temple today. For if He looked up to His mother and said, "Did you not know that I must be in My Father's house?" (Luke 2:49), He could easily turn to us and say, "And you, too, remember your Creator in the days of your youth."

But it was not Jesus who said it. It was a writer many years before Jesus who wrote it. It was Jesus who kept the saying for us. And if we would be Christlike and take to ourselves all that Christ was and is for us, then it would be well for us to pay attention to this injunction.

To Forget the Creator Is Fatal

Not to remember your Creator in the days of your youth is to jeopardize your own existence. To live one's days

54

without the Creator is not to live at all, so says Ecclesiastes, the Preacher. He is represented as Solomon, who as an old man has learned all there is to know about life. It was Solomon who began the movement of the wisdom literature. As his father had begun the collection of the psalms, the worship literature of Israel, Solomon began the collection of the wisdom literature, such as we find in the Book of Proverbs. Solomon took upon himself the role of the cultured king, the ruler who would provide for his people the wisdom literature that would create dialog with other nations and would rival them in every way.

But the Book Ecclesiastes is to serve as a corrective for all other wisdom literature. The author asserts that everything is vanity, nothingness, emptiness. Everything is foolish, absurd, and unprofitable. He is weary of life. It is always the same old thing. Nothing is ever new. As king in Jerusalem he had searched out wisdom and found that it was a striving after wind. He tried the pleasures of life, and that, too, ended as vanity. Wealth and great pleasures, health and prosperity — all were vanity. Therefore a man can do no better than "to eat and drink and find enjoyment in his toil." (Eccl. 2:24)

All of this preachment from beginning to end represents the most skeptical piece of writing in all of Scripture. And one could possibly add that it is one of the most skeptical pieces in all of literature. It is a story of cynicism and great despair. There is no appeal here to the great covenant which God had made with His people Israel. There is no introduction of a great word which had come from God. Instead the preacher makes his pronouncements and his observations on the basis of His own bitter experiences. He does not play the role of a prophet or of a priest. He appears to be the disillusioned philosopher who has grown weary of trying to figure things out. Whenever one tries to penetrate the great mysteries of life, whenever one appears on the verge of a solution, the answers slip away and one finds himself again in the midst of nothingness.

And what after all is the fate of man? Of all men? The fate of man, whether he is righteous or wicked, just or unjust, saint or sinner, is the same. All die. Just as dumb animals, they all die. All come from the dust and all return to the dust. They come from nothingness and they apparently return to nothingness. And while they live, death stalks them at every turn. Therefore it is good to remember your Creator in the days of your youth. When you are growing old, it will be exceedingly difficult to do so. The text states that the mourners are already waiting in the street for you. They are everywhere about you. And what we call life is filled with so much oppression and apparent injustice, so much pain and unsolved sorrow, it would even appear that the dead are much more fortunate than the living.

Life then without God, though it be filled with wisdom, health, and wealth, ends in despair and utter cynicism. The Preacher's cynicism is reechoed in the writings of men like Pascal and Kierkegaard, who see that the chief fault of man is that he is quite unwilling to see how desperate his situation is and unwilling to give up trying to find the answer in his own resources.

If we would be wise, it would be well for us to assess our situation properly now. It is important to know that, whatever vocation we are pursuing in life, all will be empty and vain unless we remember the Creator now at the beginning of our maturity. And it is in our vocation that He greets us.

The Creator Gives Us Hope

However, we must remember, too, that the Preacher is not all cynicism. His cynicism is meant for all attempts to live life without a remembrance of the Creator. But he now is a believer in the Creator. And he urges a simple faith upon us. He is set against the theologies and philosophies that appear to be profound, that appear to plumb the depths of the mysteries of the universe and all of history. The fact of the matter is, not all the mysteries are open to us and will not be in this life. What is needed is a faith that sees God involved in all of life as Creator. This is a faith that knows the presence of God in one's work and one's vocation. It is a faith that knows the presence of the Creator in one's suffering and pain, that knows the presence of God in the death that comes to all.

What one has to experience then by this kind of faith is the sense of creatureliness, that we are creatures and that God is God, the Creator. It is in Him that we find the answer to our existence, to our being, to our life. He gives all and He sustains all. The Preacher would urge us to take that which God gives in simple faith and live our lives in Him, find the pleasure of our labor as living and working unto Him.

Beyond this the Preacher does not go. If there is a note of redemption in this book, it is on this rather basic and simple line of thought. The nature of faith which we hear here is that we finally bow our heads before the Creator in full admission that life without Him is vanity and that we are perfectly willing to take life as He manages it for us.

But this does take us back to the holy Gospel for this day.

For the Christ is One who did remember God in the days of His youth. Already as a lad He has this sense of vocation, of finding pleasure in one's calling no matter how difficult it might be. A boy involved in the difficult work of matching questions and answers with theologians finds pleasure in it. He prefers this to playing ball on the street or carousing on the way home. His preachment contained much of what is to be found in the Preacher. He continually called for men to give up the search for their existence in their own resources. He called for a simple and childlike trust in God as Father. He reminded the people of their creatureliness and asked them to be even more so, like birds of the air and flowers of the field.

Jesus lived His life in disdain of everything that the people of His day valued. He lived His life in fearlessness of the threats they made on His life. He died in the confidence that His Father, the Creator, would raise Him from the dead. And by so doing He brought redemption for all of us who have failed to give our lives into His hands. By His life and death Jesus gave ample witness to us that God as Creator is utterly trustworthy and that He is willing to set aside our sins of unfaithfulness and rebellion against His role as Creator and Ruler of all things.

For us then to remember God as Creator is also to know Him as Redeemer. And how shall we remember Him? How shall we ground our lives in Him? How shall we anchor ourselves in Him? By surrendering to Him. By yielding to Him by faith. And what shall this surrender be? What are the terms of surrender? What is asked of us? The sign in the restaurant is appropriate: "Don't just do something. Stand there." We are called to stand still and let God speak to us.

In His Word God speaks to us of what we are and what we can be. In that Word He tells us that all need not be vanity and emptiness. In that Word and in His sacraments He will make us like unto Himself. He will fashion us out of love and grace and re-create us in the image of His Firstborn.

The Year of the Lord's Favor

The Spirit of the Lord God is upon Me, because the Lord has anointed Me to bring good tidings to the afflicted; He has sent Me to bind up the brokenhearted, to proclaim liberty to the captives, and the opening of the prison to those who are bound; to proclaim the year of the Lord's favor, and the day of vengeance of our God; to comfort all who mourn; to grant to those who mourn in Zion — to give them a garland instead of ashes, the oil of gladness instead of mourning, the mantle of praise instead of a faint spirit; that they may be called oaks of righteousness, the planting of the Lord, that He may be glorified. They shall build up the ancient ruins, they shall raise up the former devastations; they shall repair the ruined cities, the devastations of many generations. Aliens shall stand and feed your flocks, foreigners shall be your plowmen and vinedressers; but you shall be called the priests of the Lord, men shall speak of you as the ministers of our God; and you shall eat the wealth of the nations, and in their riches you shall glory.

Isaiah 61:1-6 (RSV)

⊰ The Year of the Lord's Favor ⊱

THE holy Gospel for today is the story of the first Messianic sign which our Lord performed at the wedding of Cana and manifested forth His glory. This Old Testament lesson is the text which Jesus used when He preached His first sermon in His home town Nazareth as a Rabbi. In the Gospel according to St. Luke (4:16-30) we read about that occasion. He preached this sermon at the beginning of His prophetic ministry. In this sermon He introduced the theme of His Messianic work. He announced that His task was to proclaim the year of the Lord's favor.

The Message Is of God

Our Savior employs this text to describe Himself. It was His own epiphany, His manifestation of Himself. It is the evangelist's record that very early in His ministry Jesus appears to identify Himself with the Suffering Servant of Isaiah 53. This text is a proclamation of the Servant. There was considerable question in Israel as to whether this text applied to the whole people or whether it applied to an individual servant. Jesus appears to satisfy the question by saying, "Today this scripture has been fulfilled in your hearing." This is not to say that Jesus in any way indicated that the saying had not been fulfilled by the prophet who made this proclamation for the first time or by later teachers and preachers who expounded the text properly. But He does say that He is proclaiming the year of the Lord's favor. And He did so consistently. He did so in a way that none before Him or after Him had done.

His call to proclaim the year of the Lord's favor was initiated by the Spirit of God. He could say quite properly: "The Spirit of the Lord God is upon Me, because the Lord has anointed Me to bring good tidings to the afflicted." At His baptism God had anointed the Son as the Christ "with the Holy Spirit without measure," "with the Oil of Gladness above His fellows." As kings and priests had been anointed in Israel for their calling, He was anointed with the Holy Spirit. He had been chosen, selected, anointed, marked, and sent for this special mission. He was God's Servant. But not only did He fulfill the identity of one sent by God on this mission of proclamation, He also fulfilled all the marks of the Suffering Servant. By His suffering and death He fulfilled the marks of the Servant in a special and unique sense.

However, while this text has become especially dear to Christendom because of our Lord's use of it to set His credentials in order, it is important to note that this is not the only way in which Jesus expounded the text. Nor did the prophets before Him use it simply to gain authority for their message. The authority of the text rested in the heart of the One who sent them and the One who sent the Christ. What was important about this message of the year of the Lord's favor was that it was filled with His Spirit, that it was a word come from God. This was not to be a word about God, some speculation about Him, nor yet some work contrived by those who knew God. It was a word from God sent on a mission to announce His decisive action among His people.

So we do well to listen to this word about God's year of favor, to hear it as a word from God directed to our hearts to win our love and our affection for Him who loves us with an everlasting love.

God Initiates the Action

The second observation which we can make about the proclamation of the Lord's favor is that it is the proclamation of what is already settled in the heart of God. It is God who sends the Servant. It is God who gives the word, the action that is to be proclaimed. The nature of what is to be proclaimed reveals the heart of God. The Servant is to bring good tidings to the afflicted, to bind up the broken-hearted, proclaim liberty to the captives, open the prison to those who are bound, comfort all who mourn, give a garland instead of ashes, the oil of gladness instead of mourning, the mantle of praise instead of a faint spirit. In His heart God has already decided the issue. Man is not to be left in his despair. He is not to be left in his anxiety. He is not to be bound by his sin. He is not to be left in the prison of his guilt. He is not to be drowned in the tears of his mourning for his own death. Instead God will crown His children with a garland of praise instead of the ashes they deserve.

God decided this. God decided to take the action. God desired to make it so. And God sent His prophets to cheer His people exiled and imprisoned with this good news: God has not forsaken you. The people who deserved this punishment are to hear: God has not given you up. God still claims you as His own. Cheer up. God has put aside your sin, your guilt, and your death. Live in the light of His love, covered with the garland of His praise of you as His son.

We know this action of God best in Christ. There we can see it plainly and clearly. God did not give up on His Son Jesus, who came to live in the world of our sin and our death. Instead He raised Christ from the dead. Just so in Christ God has not given up on humanity. Instead in Christ He declares that He is willing to raise up all men from the dead unto Himself. So then this word of God that comes to us in the proclamation of the year of the Lord's favor is not advice or counsel, but it is liberation, it is an act in which we are set free. It is a word that frees us from ourselves and our death.

The Message Is for the Captives

It is important for us to note that this is liberating news for those who are held captive. The proclamation of the year of the Lord's favor is totally meaningless for those who do not know that they are in bondage. The best illustration of this is found in the account of our Lord's preaching on this text in his home synagog. After He had finished preaching, they all looked at Him in great wonder. They "all spoke well of Him and wondered at the gracious words which proceeded out of His mouth" (Luke 4:22). No doubt some of them said, "I knew him when he was in school." The women may have said, "My, didn't Mary's son do fine! I always said he should be a rabbi." And some did ask, "Is not this the son of Joseph, the carpenter? How is it that he thinks he should talk this way?" And amid all this acclamation and wonderment Jesus rose to speak harsh words.

They liked His pretty and gracious words all right, but now they would want Him to perform great works among them. This He could not do, because they did not get the point. A prophet is without honor in his own country. The reason was plain. They liked gracious words, but they did not see how they applied to them. They were not the captives. They had no reason to mourn. So Jesus reminded them of an awful truth: "There were many widows in Israel in the days of Elijah . . . when there came a great famine over all the land; and Elijah was sent to none of them but only to Zarephath, in the land of Sidon, to a woman who was a widow. And there were many lepers in Israel in the time of the prophet Elisha, and none of them was cleansed but only Naaman the Syrian" (Luke 4:25-27). The word of grace and the sign of God's redeeming love came to those outside Israel. What Christ was saying is that God can help none except those who need the help and know they need the help. This word angered the people of Nazareth, and they forced Him out of the synagog and took him out to the edge of town to throw Him down from the hill to kill Him; but He escaped from them.

It is for us to note that these gracious words are not for us unless we know and confess that we are the despondent, the anxious, the sin-laden, guilt-filled, imprisoned, and dying generation who have no other help than the help which our God sends in His beloved Son. If we do not know this, then these words are words that will come to haunt us when we come to our extremities and it is too late to try them, to believe them, or to die by them.

We cannot say yes to these gracious words unless we know that by virtue of our own helplessness we are in need of grace. We cannot be liberated unless we know that we are in need of liberation. We cannot be praised of God as His sons unless we know first that we have been the children of wrath. But need we look far to see our need of this grace? We see the symbols and signs of our futility everywhere about us in the shabby pages of history we are writing for the next generation to read, in our literature of despair, in the frank confessions of bewilderment and confusion.

This is the year of the Lord's favor. Now is the hour for us, the captives and the brokenhearted, to receive from God's favor the gift of His love and grace.

God Makes Us Priests

Finally we may also observe that the year of the Lord's favor is the time of His restoration of His people as the priests of God. The prophet says: "You shall be called the priests of the Lord, men shall speak of you as the ministers of our God." In Exodus Israel had been called to be a kingdom of priests (Ex. 19:6). Now Israel would be called a nation of priests as of old. The New Testament church after the ascension of our Lord recalled these words. Peter called the people of God a royal priesthood.

To stand in the year of the Lord's favor means that we may exercise our rights and duties with only Christ as our Mediator. We have direct access to our Father in heaven with no need for sacrifices but only to offer ourselves as a living sacrifice. We may make direct intercession to Him. We may appeal daily to our baptismal covenant, come directly to His altar to receive His body and blood, hear, study, and learn daily His gracious Word to us.

Shall we then not do so? It does us little good to criticize the priestly system of other churches if we fail to exercise ourselves in the privileges and prerogatives of the royal priesthood. This would be the worst abuse of the priesthood. Then God has wasted it upon us. Rather let us avail ourselves of the means which He has placed at our disposal in a faithful and intense way. Let us live as the priests of the Lord in this year of His favor.

◆§ *Naaman, commander of the army of the king of Syria, was a great man with his master and in high favor because by him the Lord had given victory to Syria. He was a mighty man of valor, but he was a leper. Now the Syrians on one of their raids had carried off a little maid from the land of Israel, and she waited on Naaman's wife. She said to her mistress, "Would that my lord were with the prophet who is in Samaria! He would cure him of his leprosy." So Naaman went in and told his lord, "Thus and so spoke the maiden from the land of Israel." And the king of Syria said, "Go now, and I will send a letter to the king of Israel."*

So he went, taking with him ten talents of silver, six thousand shekels of gold, and ten festal garments. And he brought the letter to the king of Israel, which read, "When this letter reaches you, know that I have sent to you Naaman my servant that you may cure him of his leprosy." And when the king of Israel read the letter, he rent his clothes and said, "Am I God, to kill and to make alive, that this man sends word to me to cure a man of his leprosy? Only consider and see how he is seeking a quarrel with me."

But when Elisha the man of God heard that the king of Israel had rent his clothes, he sent to the king, saying, "Why have you rent your clothes? Let him come now to me that he may know that there is a prophet in Israel." So Naaman came with his horses and chariots and halted at the door of Elisha's house. And Elisha sent a messenger to him, saying, "Go and wash in the Jordan seven times, and your flesh shall be restored, and you shall be clean." But Naaman was angry and went away, saying, "Behold, I thought that he would surely come out to me and stand and call on the name of the Lord his God and wave his hand over the place and cure the leper. Are not Abana and Pharpar, the rivers of Damascus, better than all the waters of Israel? Could I not wash in them and be clean? So he turned and went away in a rage. But his servants came near and said to him, "My father, if the prophet had commanded you to do some great thing, would you not have done it? How much rather, then, when he says to you, 'Wash and be clean?'" So he went down and dipped himself seven times in the Jordan according to the word of the man of God; and his flesh was restored like the flesh of a little child, and he was clean.

Then he returned to the man of God, he and all his company, and he came and stood before him; and he said, "Behold, I know that there is no God in all the earth but in Israel; so accept now a present from your servant." ক

2 Kings 5:1-15 (RSV)

✑ *The Greater Work* ✑

THE grand theme which runs through the season of the Epiphany of our Lord is that He is revealed as the Son of God. The emphasis of the season is highlighted through the work which Jesus performs. This work calls for and produces faith in those who witness. It is this production of faith which is important. The work which is revealed is never the kind of work which needs no faith. Rather the faith which is produced is the faith which discerns the work as a sign of God's Messianic action.

This is an important distinction to make. How much Christian breath and ink have been wasted in the attempt to explain the possibility of God's work, to make miracles intellectually responsible, to give some kind of rational basis to a reporting of the great and mighty acts of God! We always stand in danger of falling into the trap of making the miracles attractive and believable. But this is really to miss the point. For the miracle stories are in no way related to demonstrate some kind of proof of God. If this were so, then the call of the stories would not be to faith in God but to faith in the miracles. And if someone could give a scientific basis or explanation to the miracles, then there would be no need for faith. The miracle stories are actually presented to give us a graphic description of the behavior of faith and to show us that faith is the great work.

In the Old Testament lesson for today the story of the healing of the leper Naaman, the Syrian, is an excellent story of what the heart expects to find as God's work and what it discovers by faith. The heart always expects the lesser work of God. This is certainly obvious in the case of Naaman. Naaman occupied the high position in the Syrian government of commander in chief of the army. He had been favored by his king. He had been feted for his valor and his victories. But he was a leper. His prestige, his wealth, and his honor were meaningless for want of his health. A nameless girl who was taken in one of the Syrian raids of the Northern Kingdom of Israel told about the prophet in her homeland who could heal him. The king of Syria concurs in the idea that Naaman should go to the prophet. He sends along an imperial letter commanding the king of Israel to have his servant healed. The king of Israel is terrified, but Elisha sends word that Naaman should come to him. Naaman goes. But he is utterly disappointed. The prophet doesn't come out to him but sends word by his servant that Naaman should dip himself in the Jordan seven times.

Naaman had come prepared to put his full confidence in the prophet. He came loaded with gifts of money and festal garments. The money alone had an extremely high cash value. He had come prepared to pay a premium price. People will do that. They are willing to seek out any and every resource they can. They will hunt up the quacks. They will search out the best. They will make no differentiation between the faith healer, the professional person, or the quack. Desperation is incapable of discernment. The man who desires to preserve his life, the man who lives on tenterhooks, is quite willing to turn over the last sliver of his life to anyone at all who gives the slightest hope that he will nourish it and make it strong again. So came Naaman, imperial letter in hand, servants carrying an enormous sum of money, and willingness in his own heart to have the prophet in Israel work a great miracle upon him. Small wonder he was disappointed.

Is that kind of disappointment familiar to you? You have heard and read about people who throng to the faith healers, waiting and hoping for the faith healer to work the great work upon them. They wait for the faith healer to do what Naaman claimed Elisha failed to do. "I thought that he would surely come out to me and stand and call on the name of the Lord his God and wave his hand over the place and cure the leper." You see, the formula is a common one, a natural one, the one that people expect. They want the magical incantations, they want the miraculous to happen with all the trappings of some pious phrases and some dramatic action. And don't we expect the same thing? We come to God prepared to be cured of our sin or our sins. We come with our good intentions in hand, loaded down with our willingness to pay a price, even with witnesses to our good intentions. And we wait for the spectacular to happen. We want the magic touch, the sonorous soundings of piety, the obvious act of power and glory that will suddenly transform us. But it doesn't happen. And because it doesn't happen, we are apt to think that God has failed, that the church has failed, and that we have wasted our energy in coming to God.

Or in reflecting on what is prescribed, disappointment may be of another nature. When Naaman considered only what was asked of him, he thought this totally and completely irrational. He was to go and dip himself seven times in the Jordan River. This was absolutely out of the question. What good could that possibly do? If he had to dip himself in water, the clearer and more beneficial streams of his own country would be more logical. The Jordan was the last place he could look to for healing. That river was nothing but dark muddied waters cutting between banks of mud. His servants reminded him that he had come prepared to do anything. Yet he felt this completely out of the question. He would gladly have paid more money than he had brought. He would have been willing to give up his career if the prophet had so prescribed. He would have crawled on the ground, done any kind of penance necessary. Ask any act, any vow, a conversion to the Hebrew way of life, anything — anything but this!

This is not too unlike our own feelings when we would have God recognize our willingness to be healed of our sin. If He will not perform the great act that would suddenly and gloriously transform us in a very obvious way, then let us take over. Let us work the works that would gain His favor. There are days when we would gladly and willingly crawl down this aisle to this chancel, when we would gladly have God ask anything of us, and in penitence we would do it. If in our penitence we could buy His favor, we would lay the price on the line. We would gladly learn the Jesus prayer like Franny Glass in *Franny and Zooey,* who thinks that the incessant repetition of an ancient prayer will help her achieve a pious life. If that would work holiness for us, we would incant it from this day forward. But God strangely and silently turns away from all our offers. He refuses to pay attention to such self-centered piety. He would work the work in us. A splashy show of power is a lesser work that would not last. Our works, too, would be lesser works that could avail us little. God waits to perform the greater work.

God Performs the Greater Work

The greater work is and always will be faith. Naaman happily learned this. He took the advice of the servants and did as Elisha prescribed through his servant. He gathered up his group and made the pilgrimage to Jordan. There he dipped himself in the water seven times and was cured. But a greater miracle was wrought in him that day. He had been brought to faith. Faith had its beginnings when Naaman, against his better judgment, with absolutely no confidence in the purifying waters of the Jordan, was obedient to the word which he had received from Elisha. Then having found healing, he was enraptured by the confidence which he had in Elisha's God. He had been led to see the greater work — faith in the God who healed, not in the healing.

Naaman was one day to die. But what he found by faith that day was to sustain him even through death. It was by the Word, a word from God, an action of God, that Naaman was saved that day. You find the parallel to this story in the holy Gospel for today. Here a leper is cleansed because he comes to Jesus and says, "Lord, if You will, You can make me clean." And Jesus stretched out His hand and touched him, saying, "I will; be clean." In this case the man had the faith to begin with: "Lord, if You will, You can make me clean." Which is also to say, "Lord, if You will, You can make me clean; but if You don't, You are still Lord." Jesus, however, cleansed him that this faith might be confirmed. But it was again the word that was the healing, not the touching, for the man did not know that

Jesus would touch him. Rather he believed in Jesus. In the case of the centurion at Capernaum the parallel is even more obvious. He says, "Lord, I am not worthy to have You come under my roof; but *only say the word* and my servant will be healed." Again it is by the power of the Word that the miraculous is wrought. This is the greater work — the work of faith which trusts the Word of God.

Can you not see how this is all related to your own spiritual healing? In the case of Naaman we may paraphrase the word of your catechetical training in the meaning of Baptism: "It was indeed not the waters of the Jordan that effected this great healing but the word of God which was in and with the dirty waters of the Jordan; for without the word of God from Elisha that water would have been simple muddy water and no healing, but with the word of God it was a healing and a gracious water of life."

Naaman's story is your story and mine. For it is in Holy Baptism that we are called to faith. There God gives us the assurance that we are healed in a special sense. As the greater work for Naaman was his faith, so this is and always shall be the greater work which God performs in our lives. To be sure, day by day God shall perform works in our lives. The problem with this is that we are not always able to recognize them or that one person is able to recognize them in a greater or lesser degree than another. But what is common to us all is our Holy Baptism, wherein God has given the assurance of His saving mercy. We need look for no other act that would prove mightier or greater than this. For this is it. In this gracious water of life He gives the pledge of His love and forgiveness. In effect He draws us into the life of Jesus Christ, into His death, into His resurrection. Just as the story relates that Naaman was cleansed by the waters connected with the prophet's word, so we are cleansed by this water that is connected with the Word and life of Jesus Christ.

It bears repeating. Naaman died. But on the day that he found faith in the God of Elisha, his cleansing became a pledge of God's faithfulness to him for eternity. And so also at our Baptism God gives us the pledge that He shall raise us unto life eternal.

That is the greater work — the work of faith, the work that calls us to take full advantage of God's mercy to all eternity.

God Saves His People

⋙ "The Lord will fight for you, and you have only to be still." The Lord said to Moses, "Why do you cry to Me? Tell the people of Israel to go forward. Lift up your rod, and stretch out your hand over the sea and divide it that the people of Israel may go on dry ground through the sea. And I will harden the hearts of the Egyptians so that they shall go in after them, and I will get glory over Pharaoh and all his host, his chariots, and his horsemen. And the Egyptians shall know that I am the Lord when I have gotten glory over Pharaoh, his chariots, and his horsemen." Then the Angel of God who went before the host of Israel moved and went behind them; and the pillar of cloud moved from before them and stood behind them, coming between the host of Egypt and the host of Israel. And there was the cloud and the darkness; and the night passed without one coming near the other all night. Then Moses stretched out his hand over the sea; and the Lord drove the sea back by a strong east wind all night and made the sea dry land, and the waters were divided. ⋙

Exodus 14:14-21

⋯ God Saves His People ⋯

ONE of the religious questions raised with great frequency is, How can I know for sure that God is in my life? The question is raised seriously. People would like to have some evidence, a point of referral, a significant moment which may be interpreted readily as an act of God for them.

In the Old Testament Lesson for today, the story of the Exodus, and in the holy Gospel for today, the Stilling of the Tempest, we have related lessons which reveal actions of God. And your first reaction to these might be: "Yes, if I were there to witness those events, it would be easy for me to believe. But things like that don't happen in my life, and that's why I have such a hard time believing."

Yet if we were to look at these stories carefully, we should change our mind and we should see that God continues to work among us.

God Acts in History

When we look at this Old Testament story, it is clear to us that this is an act of history. This is a story of a people. It is the story of a people of bondage, a weak people under the domination of powerful and glorious Egypt. It is a story not unlike those of modern world history. One may liken the situation to the relationship between East Germany and the Soviet government, like a rising nationalist power of

Africa trying to throw off the shackles of a colonial power, or like the relationship between the Jews and Nazi Germany. These people of Israel had suffered tyranny under Egypt. Their infant sons had been slain in ruthless fashion to keep down the population. They had been existing under the shackles of slave labor. They had been given the hope of liberation only to have it taken away from them nine different times. On those nine occasions Moses had interpreted to the Pharaoh that nine plagues which had come to Egypt were signs from God that Pharaoh should let the people go. Finally, in the midst of the awful terror that brought death to Egypt, Pharaoh decided to let the people go. After they left, he moved in hot pursuit of them with his army.

The Children of Israel came to the Red Sea. Here they are dispirited and dejected. But that night an east wind blew all night, dried the land, and the Children of Israel crossed over on dry ground. Just at the moment when the people were at the height of despair they believed that God acted on their behalf. At a time when it was extremely vivid that they could not help themselves, God helped them. At a time when they were absolutely dependent, God was their Benefactor. It was in a crisis — a crisis that does occur to the peoples and nations — that God acted, that He performed a great act.

Now God acts that way in the lives of men, of you and me. He may perform His mighty deeds upon a nation, upon a community, upon the individual. But most generally it is true that God's most decisive action, His most obvious work, is evident when people are in definite need of Him. People can discern His hand in history, or they can see Him at work in their own lives when they are despondent, when they have been brought low, when they are in suffering and despair. This is not to say that this is the only way in which people may become sensitive to the need of the presence of God. But it is to say that it is seldom or infrequent that they are conscious of His presence without being brought to a sense of utter dependency.

What is important for us is that God dealt with this situation at the Red Sea in the manner in which He did. The text states that God made an east wind blow all night and dry the land. I am not going to list the thousand and one stories that came out of World War II to parallel this story. There are stories of how the wind changed to help the Allies, how snow covered the tracks of the scouts of the Allies, how rain came at the right moment, or how birds landed on rafts to provide a meal for the shipwrecked at sea. I will leave it to you to sort out the hundreds of war stories that men relate to testify to the mighty working of God or to give evidence that God had His hand in their battle. That's what the Exodus story is. It is a war story that recounts how God used an east wind to make conditions favorable for the escape of the Children of Israel. They were so impressed with this action that they never forgot it, and they rehearse the memory of it every year at their celebration of the Passover. This event to them is what the Christ event is for us Christians.

God delivered Israel by a wind. The New Testament church sees that He delivered us by a Man. That Man appeared to be so ordinary that His relatives and His neighbors refused to believe on Him. He was a Man so ordinary that the Gospel recounts that when some would believe on Him, others would ask, "But isn't this Mary's son?" or, "Isn't this Joseph's son?"

On what appears to be the ordinary, what appears to

be the commonplace or the natural, God performs His mighty acts. By a wind He saved a people, by a Man He saved mankind.

So if it is God you are looking for, if it is some great act you are waiting for Him to perform, do not look for Him or His action in the extraordinary, but look for Him in the ordinary. He meets you in the daily walk of life. He seeks you out in your everyday vocation, in your classroom, in your home, in the daily broadcasts, in the daily routine. And He will perform His mighty acts in the mean and the little, with the natural and the profane.

God Creates Faith

Therefore this is not where we leave the story. To be sure, both the Old and the New Testament of Scripture are consistent in revealing the mighty acts of God as His dealings with people in the natural environs of their history. But the Scriptures are not simply a recital of the acts of God, they are also the account of man's reaction to God's action in history. It is so in this instance also.

When the Children of Israel were so desperate about their situation, their hearts were changed into hearts of joy and faith by this mighty act. When they crossed over into safety, they discerned that this was a saving and redeeming act of God. God had saved them. God was to be worshiped and honored as a redeeming God. They trusted and believed on Him. This act pointed beyond the crossing of the sea. This act pointed to a greater and more glorious deliverance which this God could make. So the men of faith, by faith and through faith interpreted this action of God to be for their welfare and their salvation.

Not so Pharaoh's troops. They saw the same act, the same deed. They must have been just as astounded and just as excited. After all that had happened in Egypt, the kind of testimony which Moses had given, one would think that the command should have been given: "Let them go, boys. We've had it. They have a God on their side who makes even the winds and the waves obey Him. Let us worship this God of Israel. We have no god like Him." But they didn't. They decided to pursue Israel and to cross where the Israelites had passed. But, the text says, "they drove heavily." They bogged down in the mud. Wheels came off. The pillar of cloud that was between them and the Israelites affected them. They were in a fog. Finally they do cry out, "Let us flee from before Israel, for the Lord fights for them against the Egyptians." But it was too late!

So here then is the point. As God confronts us in our everyday situation, as He greets us in history, as He performs His mighty acts in the natural environs, as He comes to us in the ordinary, everyday situations, we have to react for Him or against Him.

The way in which He has greeted all of us is in Jesus Christ. In the story of Christ, in the proclamation of Christ, in His Word, in His sacraments God performs a mighty and great act for us. He saves us. He saves us from destroying ourselves. He rescues us. He saves us from seeing that life is living on the terms of this world. In Jesus Christ God enables us to see beyond this life. By the death and resurrection of Jesus Christ God enables us to look into the tomorrow of eternity. He spares us the agony of believing that this is all there is to life. In the proclamation of Christ, God grants us freedom from a life that is death. That is the story. But it is more than story. It is your life.

Every day that you walk to work or to class you are going to confront situations that will depend solely and completely on what you believe about your God and what He has revealed about Himself in the Lord Jesus Christ. Every day the Christ even will be new to you in the way that you see your situation.

To put it backwards, think of it this way: On the day that the Israelites were delivered by God, they were happy. They felt saved. They believed on God and His servant Moses. But the very next time they faced a difficulty they forgot all about God and did not believe. The lapses of faith occurred so frequently that the apostle Paul says none of them reached the Promised Land because of their unbelief.

The parallel story is in the holy Gospel for today. When the boat is tossed by a storm, the disciples forget in their anxiety the mighty acts which Christ had performed for them. Jesus calls them people of little faith.

It is against this kind of unbelief and unfaith that God works. God has performed His great and mighty act for us in Jesus Christ. He has made us His own. There is no reason for us to fear. It is in Christ that He gives us the clues for understanding the way in which He deals and works with us each day. Each day is filled with the natural and commonplace events of the normal routine. Nevertheless in Christ we know He is present, working and doing to transform our little lives by His mighty acts of love.

❧ *And you, son of man, say to the house of Israel, Thus have you said: "Our transgressions and our sins are upon us, and we waste away because of them; how then can we live?" Say to them, As I live, says the Lord God, I have no pleasure in the death of the wicked but that the wicked turn from his way and live; turn back, turn back from your evil ways; for why will you die, O house of Israel? And you, son of man, say to your people, The righteousness of the righteous shall not deliver him when he transgresses; and as for the wickedness of the wicked, he shall not fall by it when he turns from his wickedness; and the righteous shall not be able to live by his righteousness when he sins. Though I say to the righteous that he shall surely live, yet if he trusts in his righteousness and commits iniquity, none of his righteous deeds shall be remembered; but in the iniquity that he has committed he shall die. Again, though I say to the wicked, "You shall surely die," yet if he turns from his sin and does what is lawful and right, if the wicked restores the pledge, gives back what he had taken by robbery, and walks in the statutes of life, committing no iniquity, he shall surely live, he shall not die. None of the sins that he has committed shall be remembered against him; he has done what is lawful and right, he shall surely live.* ❧

Ezekiel 33:10-16 (RSV)

⊷ *God's Patience* ⊷

O UR time calls for great patience. We cannot even enjoy the peace that exists between the two great power blocs of the world. We live by coexistence in a cold war. We know full well that what keeps our war cold is a nuclear stalemate that must be fed by frantic stockpiling of nuclear weapons that in turn threaten the stalemate. In the meantime we hope that patience and understanding can transform and convert the situation through deliberate and lasting solutions.

One cynical editor has suggested the hope that the stalemate would last long enough for the other world power to catch up with us economically so that they could be as soft as we and thus become less aggressive. That kind of hope calls for patience too.

But the sensitive soul is more likely to wonder how long God in His good patience can tolerate our situation. History does not deal gently with nations who suddenly become hysterical about the art of self-preservation. And for one who understands history in the light of God's reign, the question is not only: Can we as nations be patient with one another? but: Can God be patient with us?

The similar question was raised by the Children of Israel in their captivity. It was the prophet Ezekiel who handled the question.

God Shows His Concern

It should be of great comfort for man to know that God is concerned with man's ultimate questions about himself and about his destiny. The prophet Ezekiel made it his task to make this proclamation to the Children of Israel. When the Children of Israel had failed to discern the hand of God in their history, when they were indifferent to the covenant relationship which God had established with them, this prophet forewarned them of the inevitable doom that awaited them. The prophet issued the warning that Israel was destroying itself. Destruction and captivity were inevitable so long as the people paid no attention to the Word which God had given to His people. In eloquent language he signaled the imminent destruction of Israel.

But now Israel had experienced her doom. The nation had been brought low. Her children were in exile. She acknowledged her sin. In retrospect the people of captivity could say that her prophets had been right. They should have listened to the voice of the men from God. But the question for her now was: "Our transgressions and our sins are upon us, and we waste away because of them; how then can we live?" So the people spoke to the prophet. Finally the people had arrived at the point of seeing their own hopelessness. Life had disintegrated into a wasting away. It was no more than this. This was not a people in abject slavery as their fathers had been in Egypt. This was not a people in prison camps of a fascist government. This was not a people behind an iron curtain. From what we know of the Captivity, these people had known a freedom in their exile that enabled them to keep their identity. The Hebrews were given the privilege of maintaining their own laws, their own schools, their own academies. They were given the privilege of entering into commerce and maintaining their own businesses. Later one was even appointed to the fourth rank in the empire as the "Prince of the Captivity."

Yet the children of the Captivity mourned in their dirgeful psalm: By the rivers of Babylon, there we sat down, yea, we wept when we remembered Zion (Ps. 137:1). They had been humbled because they had lost their purpose as a people of God. They had lost life. They had been cut off from their lineage with God. They could envision no fulfillment of the great covenant which God had made with them. They had mocked and destroyed their own destiny.

But God was not insensitive to their weeping and their lament. In His great patience God waited for this moment when they were ready to say that they were wasting away. So God waits for us in our day. We are captives to a life of which we, too, must say, "Our transgressions and our sins are upon us, and we waste away because of them; how then can we live?" We live in a land of affluence that would have made the previous generations envious. We have solved an endless variety of problems that plagued our grandfathers, and yet we must confess that "we waste away" in the face of the enormous problems we have created. Immorality has gotten completely out of hand. Our ability to create monsters of destruction is out of control. We have manufactured an industrial society that becomes more meaningless day by day. We have distilled emptiness and phoniness in the culture in a desperate attempt to find something to live for.

But God is patient. He waits for us to say it: "Our transgressions and our sins are upon us, and we waste away because of them; how then can we live?"

God Shows His Patience

God patiently waited for His people to confess their spiritual bankruptcy. When they did, His prophet was ready to speak a word to them, a word of comfort and of hope, a word that reinforced God's covenant with His people: "As I live, says the Lord God, I have no pleasure in the death of the wicked but that the wicked turn from his way and live; turn back, turn back from your evil ways; for why will you die, O house of Israel?" This is not a simple word, a pleasant wish, a pious hope of God. It is an oath, a pledge, a solemn, holy, and righteous declaration in which God pledges His own life. God does not want His creatures to die. He takes no pleasure, no satisfaction, no delight, no revenge in seeing His creatures die, creatures into whom He has poured the gift of life. To witness death is painful for God.

How painful for God it is to witness the death of His creatures we learn in the life of our Lord Jesus Christ! In Christ God makes good His oath and His pledge. In the tears of Christ it is God who weeps. In the mourning of Christ it is God who mourns. In the death of Christ it is God who gives His life that men might know that He takes no pleasure in their death. And He takes His life again in the resurrection that all men might know that in Him they may find their life again.

For the Children of Israel the prophet's word was to be a new declaration of hope, a word of promise that they would be returned to their land, that Jerusalem would be rebuilt, that they would stand again in the sanctuary of their heavenly Father. For us the word means that there is also hope. In the Christ our lives can be made new again. In the Christ we can be restored as the children of God.

God's Word is the promise of restoration, of regeneration, of new hope. To turn back to God is to turn back to life. In Him we shall not waste away, but we shall live. In Him we can rise above the threats of the nuclear stalemate, the slavery to a world of things, the decadence of a world of sensuality. We can live in the midst of all this sure-fire death because we may walk in the hope that the living God has no pleasure in our death.

Yet the word does not end here. The prophet joyfully and sympathetically speaks God's oath of salvation to the people, but he adds words which are to govern the relationship between God and His people. This is the restoration of the covenant between God and His people as of old. The terms are the same. God by His grace will be the saving God of this people. He will deliver them from their plight. He will fulfill His promises to them. He will save them from death. He will be their Redeemer. God will act for His people. He will be their God and they will be His people. But now, as at the giving of the Law at Sinai, the people are to pledge themselves to God in faith by doing His will. Yet in this instance the conditions are stated more explicitly as to what shall happen when man sins.

God does not become the God of His people by their keeping of the Law. Nor do they become His people by the keeping of the Law. But their doing of His will is their consistent sign that by faith they know Him as their God. So then the prophet indicates this by saying that none can make an appeal to his own righteousness when he sins. None can trust in his own righteousness for deliverance from his guilt or his death. To do so is to invite death. For life and righteousness come by God's gift. When we sin we violate that righteousness which is not ours, and therefore we can lay claim to no righteousness, and we are guilty of death.

On the other hand, God's prophet declares that when a man sins, he may appeal to God's patience, love, and grace. For even though God has declared that the sinner should die, the sinner will not die if he makes confession of his sin, makes what amends he can, and trusts God's grace. God will not remember his sins, none of the sins which he has committed, and he will live.

This is God's patience. This is His love and His grace. Patiently He waits for man to think through the questions that confront him in his dilemmas. Patiently He waits out the introspection. Patiently He waits for men to take the offer of His restoration of life through His Son, the Christ. And patiently, day in and day out, He restores the fallen to grace anew until finally He shall restore us for the last time to a life that shall need no restoration.

What shall we do with this patient God? Daily He waits to renew His covenant in Christ with us. To ignore His offer of life is to trust our own righteousness, which ends in death. Are we not fools to raise the question? Should we not rather eagerly feed upon His gifts of grace and readily do that which is pleasing in His sight?

A Vision of the Glory

◄§ When Moses came down from Mount Sinai, with the two tables of the testimony in his hand as he came down from the mountain, Moses did not know that the skin of his face shone because he had been talking with God. And when Aaron and all the people of Israel saw Moses, behold, the skin of his face shone, and they were afraid to come near him. But Moses called to them; and Aaron and all the leaders of the congregation returned to him, and Moses talked with them. And afterward all the people of Israel came near, and he gave them in commandment all that the Lord had spoken with him in Mount Sinai. And when Moses had finished speaking with them, he put a veil on his face; but whenever Moses went in before the Lord to speak with Him, he took the veil off until he came out; and when he came out and told the people of Israel what he was commanded, the people of Israel saw the face of Moses, that the skin of Moses' face shone; and Moses would put the veil upon his face again until he went in to speak with Him. §►

Exodus 34:29-35 (RSV)

❧ *A Vision of the Glory* ☙

W E may come to church out of habit, but each of us still has the hope of deriving some benefits from attending church worship. What we really want is a vision of the glory of God. And yet out of sheer force of habit we do make that vision unlikely. In our worship we have developed a kind of entertainment complex. The sermon must be "enjoyable," the choirs "excellent," the hymns must be "old favorites," and the organ music "well executed." Now while it is true that we have a right to expect excellence in the worship service and while it is also true that taste may also make certain features of the service difficult for us, those features should not be allowed to distort or destroy the vision for us. Where the vision is to be seen and realized, to be known and experienced, is in all that we do here, but to be able to see it and to become a part of it, we must first know what the vision of glory is.

God Gives a Glimpse of His Glory

The vision of the glory which the Children of Israel saw was through their mediator Moses. This was on that historic occasion when Moses delivered to the people the two tables of stone in restoration of the covenant which God had made with His people. At the first giving of this covenant the people had become idolatrous at the foot of the mountain which was the scene of this unique religious experience. Because of their worship of the golden calf, Moses destroyed the first tablets of the covenant, pulverized the idol, and called the people to repentance. When the stir and the commotion of that traumatic event had subsided, when the unrepentant had been purged from the camp, Moses went into the mount again to make intercession for the people in the hope of reestablishing the covenant. He made a plea for the people on the basis of God's mercy. He was willing to lay down his own life to make satisfaction for the people. God acquiesced to Moses' intercession but did not demand his life. Instead he called for obedience. God gave the promise that He would remain faithful to the people, and the people in turn were to give Him obedience. As a pledge of God's faithfulness, Moses asks God to show him His glory.

In reply God said that no one may see His glory, for His glory would consume sinful man. However, that Moses might know of God's faithfulness and have a pledge of His presence, the story relates that God conceded that Moses might have a glimpse of His back and of His cloak. He instructed Moses to stand in a cleft in the rock and God would cover him with His hand until He passed by, and then Moses would be able to see His back. It is in this extraordinary experience of God's glory that Moses received the restored covenant. He remained in the mount in this presence of God for 40 days and 40 nights without food or drink and emerged from this involvement of rhapsody and ecstasy with bounding zeal to share the restored covenant with the people.

For the people this was an event long to be remembered. In the exodus God had given substantial evidence of His willingness to be the God of this His chosen people. As a weak, uncultured, unarmed, homeless people they saw clearly that there was no other choice. But that choice gave way easily to idolatry at the first test of faith when Moses did not appear. But at the restoration of the covenant, substance was given to the faith that had so easily waned. Here God gave shape and form to the faith of His people. This people was to live in community as His people. The revelation of the covenant was to make the effect of the exodus itself an ever-present reality. God, who had delivered His people, would continually be their Deliverer. God, who had revealed Himself in power at the Red Sea, would continually reveal Himself in love. God, who had come to them in grace, would continue to come to them in grace. Thus it is that the covenant was to be the basis of the constant appeal of the prophets who were to come to speak the Word of God to this people. The Word had been mediated through the mediator Moses. It had been received in faith, and it was to be communicated from generation to generation by the faithful.

The seal and the sign of the momentous occasion had been the theophany, the revelation of God's glory. And the people themselves were to be witnesses to this sign when Moses reappeared from the mountain. The skin of his face shone with radiance, which caused the people to be fearful and afraid by reason of their sinfulness.

It was then that Moses adopted the habit of wearing a veil when he was in the presence of the people. That veil was to become a symbol of the presence of the living and holy God. Moses had reflected God's presence on that glorious occasion. However, it is the apostle Paul who tells us in his second letter to the church at Corinth that the reason Moses kept wearing the veil was that the glory actually faded away. The veil hid the fact that it had. But the veil also kept alive the memory of that theophany and kept the seal of the covenant before the people. The veil became the sign of Moses' holy office as the mediator of his people.

The veil symbolized the presence of the holy and righteous God, into which no man may dare to look. This veil was continued as the symbol in the tabernacle by the veil that hid the Holy of Holies from the people and was still later introduced into the temple. Its significance remained for the people through their history. For them it meant that they had once had a glimpse of the glory of God, the holy and righteous God who had made a covenant with them through the mediator Moses.

God Gives a Fuller Vision of His Glory

It is the Old Testament that remembers for us the truth that the Children of Israel had a glimpse of the glory of God in the face of Moses. It is the New Testament that proclaims to us that we have a steady vision of the glory of God in the face of Christ Jesus. In the Holy Gospel for today we have witness to the transfiguration of our Lord on the mount. The significance of that event was twofold. For our Lord, who entered the mount as the mediator of the New Testament, it was precisely the same pledge of faithfulness which God gave to Moses when he entered the mount as mediator. And yet it was more. For this Christ was more than the Mediator of the new covenant. He was the fulfillment of the old. He was the New Covenant. He did more than to offer Himself in death for the sins of the people. God accepted His offer, which was to be fulfilled on the cross. He did more than to radiate the glory. The glory was in Him, in His person. In Him dwelt the fullness of the Godhead. Thus for Him the transfiguration was a pledge of the Father's faithfulness to Him, a source of strength for the great ordeal of the sacrifice awaiting Him. Significantly the evangelists mention that Moses and Elijah, those great heroic figures of the old covenant, are there with Him to strengthen Him and to speak about His impending death and the promise of His resurrection.

The other persons for whom the event was significant were Peter, James, and John, the witnesses to the transfiguration. As the Children of Israel had seen the radiance in the face of Moses, the disciples saw the radiance in the Christ. For them too, it was a pledge. In the Epistle appointed for today Peter is heard to say: "We were eye-witnesses of His majesty. For when He received honor and glory from God the Father and the voice was borne to Him by the Majestic Glory . . . we were with Him on the holy mountain. And we have the prophetic Word made more sure." And in the prolog of the Gospel according to St. John: "We have beheld His glory, glory as of the only Son from the Father." Here, too, was pledge, strength, assurance for the days ahead. Here was the vision that would help them to penetrate the meaning of the cross, the empty tomb, and the ascension, a vision that would become clearer at Pentecost.

But you ask, How do we get the vision of this glory? How do we become a part of this revelation? The New Testament does not leave us without answer. The evangelists record that when our Lord died on the cross, the veil in the temple was torn asunder. God was no longer hid. His glory had been revealed in the Suffering Servant, His Son, who had fulfilled His covenant. And Paul tells us: "Through Christ is it [the veil of Moses] taken away. . . . And we all, with unveiled face beholding the glory of the Lord, are being

27831

changed into His likeness from one degree of glory to another." (2 Cor. 3:14, 18)

Martin Luther, commenting on John 1:18: "No one has ever seen God; the only Son, who is in the bosom of the Father, He has made Him known," says: "Yes, Moses himself could not behold God. . . . Thus Moses viewed God's mercy from behind, as it is seen in the divine Word. As for the rest, Moses knew what he was to do; but he was not able to see God's plan and purpose. . . . Through the only-begotten Son and through the Gospel one learns to look directly into God's face. And when this happens, then everything in man dies; man must then confess that he is a blind and ignorant sinner who must forthwith appeal to Christ. . . . The knowledge of the Gospel is the face of God, the message that we have grace and truth through the death of Christ. . . . And only he who remains in Him knows God." (*Luther's Works*, Vol. 22, pp. 157, 158)

Would you then look into the face of God? Would you desire a vision of the glory? Do you desire to be transformed when you come here on a Sunday morning? Then look for the veil. Notice there is none hiding the altar. Look to that cross. Let it remind you that God has revealed His mercy and grace in the death of our Lord. Look to that altar. Let it symbolize to you that the Christ is risen and that it stands as an empty tomb with the promise of His presence among you. Look to this pulpit and let it remind you of the proclamation of freedom which God has given you from your sins, your death, and the agony of your hell. Look to this font and let it remind you that God has drowned your sin in Christ and given you the pledge of your resurrection. Come to this altar and know that God gives you His very glory when He gives to you the body and blood of His Son.

To have the vision of glory is to look up and away from yourself, away from the tired world that holds you, away from the death that frightens and haunts you, and to know that in Christ you are God's and He is yours.

Something to Glory In

Thus says the Lord: "Let not the wise man glory in his wisdom, let not the mighty man glory in his might, let not the rich man glory in his riches; but let him who glories glory in this, that he understands and knows Me, that I am the Lord who practice kindness, justice, and righteousness in the earth; for in these things I delight, says the Lord."

Jeremiah 9:23, 24 (RSV)

☙ Something to Glory In ❧

THIS little text epitomizes the preachment of the book of the prophet Jeremiah. What circumstances were the context of this sermonic material we do not know. It may well have been that this word was written at a time when Israel had enjoyed one of those rare moments of peace and tranquillity when the powerful nations about her were not harassing her with threats. She may have been enjoying a relaxation of tensions in a cold war. Her diplomatic corps, her chiefs of staff, and her economic advisers may have been elated that they were the engineers of a lasting peace. If this were so or if the circumstances were only similar, the prophet would not let the people rest in their easy confidence. Their accomplishments were nothing to glory in. There was only one reason for man to glory in — God's covenant.

It is good for us to remember this in our age of tension and concern that is apt to continue for many years to come. In the intervening periods of relaxed tensions we need to be reminded that precisely then we should not permit our achievements to become the basis for a false glory.

What Not to Glory In

The prophet makes it quite clear what we are not to glory in. "Let not the wise man glory in his wisdom."

This is a hard saying for our generation, which believes so firmly and confidently in learning. It is a particularly hard saying for people living in an age of science and sophisticated learning. However, we should be ever so careful to explain that this saying does not despise wisdom. This is not a saying against the wise man. We should never be guilty of belittling the pursuit of knowledge. We should not berate the attempt of the university to engage itself with its full resources and vigor in the attempts to study man, his history, and the world he lives in. The university should be given full freedom to ask all the questions it will, to submerge itself in research, to test and retest, and to examine every area of life and the creation known to man. And we should never become defensive or negative about these intellectual pursuits. In fact, it is our calling to enter into the study and debate, to become inquisitive about the world and man. Every man has this calling from God, and he should not be fearful of it. He should feel free to engage himself with the leading questions of his day.

However, the point of the prophetic Word is that man is not to glory in his wisdom. He is not to make a boast of it. He is not to make himself the center of his own wisdom. His wisdom is not to be humanism. For when man makes his glory in his own knowledge about himself or about his world, he has completely degenerated wisdom. Then his knowledge is not wisdom. Then he has sinned against himself and his God. His sin against himself is that he has conceived of himself as a part of the world and no more than that. When he makes his wisdom the basis of his glory, he has fastened himself to the world and he cannot rise above it. He has destroyed his identity and his validity as a child of God. He is creature only, and like all the rest of the creation he will come to an end. He will surely die.

The wise man who glories in wisdom sins against God in that he has made wisdom his god. He is wisdom's child, not God's. And in this he becomes the child of folly and foolishness, for "the wisdom of this world is folly with God," says Paul (1 Cor. 3:19). To be wisdom's child is to know about many things, but it is to be ignorant about the "things which are not seen," to be ignorant of the God who gave us a cross to glory in and by which to save us. If any would be wise, let him know this, that "the foolishness of God is wiser than men." (1 Cor. 1:25)

The second thing we dare not glory in is might. "Let not the mighty man glory in his might." One would think that in our time every sensible man would be capable of understanding this. There was a time when the nations of history would find this offensive. The rhythm of history was sustained by powerful aggressor nations who became great by aggressive action or who maintained themselves by forceful defenses. In the later periods of history it has become more apparent, however, that sooner or later power failed them all. At the point when they became conscious of or gloried in their might, they were already on the decline. In our nuclear age it should be all the more obvious that there is absolutely no sense in glorying in might. Might is the very threat to our existence, no matter how one looks at it. Yet there would be some who will not see it that way. That strange corps of people who currently criticized the American foreign policy as a "no-win policy" were properly answered by the President of our country: "Now if someone thinks we should have a nuclear war in order to win, I can inform them that there will not be winners in the next nuclear war." (Feb. 14, 1962)

Nor can the mighty man who would glory in his might

ever win. For he, too, sins against himself and his God. He sins against himself because again he thinks that he must look to himself to win the day. And even if he should win today, tomorrow comes when all of his resources of might will fail him. Tomorrow he must die. He may win ever so many battles through the power of his might, but he will not win the war with death if he has made might his glory.

The mighty man who glories in his might sins against God in that he has made might his god. But his god will utterly fail him. He is doomed because death will rob him of his god. He has failed to glory in the God who becomes man's Strength when he is the weakest, the God "whose power is made perfect in weakness" (2 Cor. 12:9). He has failed to glory in the God who has already won the day for him by destroying the mortal enemy death by the cross of His Son Jesus Christ and has given man entrance into eternity through the empty tomb of Christ.

The third thing that we dare not glory in is riches. "Let not the rich man glory in his riches." This should be so obvious to us that we should not even have to talk about it. Yet if it is obvious, there are very few signs that men believe this seriously. There is a great deal of lip service paid to this in our time. In Tennessee Williams' play *Cat on a Hot Tin Roof* Big Daddy, wealthy but dying of cancer, confesses that the rich man buys and buys, buys everything in the hope that maybe one of his purchases might be life everlasting. But the point is that riches can buy and buy, but they can't buy the right thing. Wealth is not to be despised, but to glory in wealth is to be condemned. For the man who glories in riches has also sinned against himself and his God.

He has sinned against himself because he has deceived himself. He has handcuffed himself to his riches in the hope that they will not fail him. But fail him they will. The highest fee will not buy off death. And in the face of death the wealthiest man is bankrupt if he would hope that the god of riches would deliver him. The man who glories in his riches has sinned against his God because God would gladly have given him the pearl of great price, would gladly have given him treasures in the storehouse of eternity, where moth and rust do not corrupt and thieves do not break through and steal. (Matt. 6:20)

In brief, what the prophet has to say to us is that we cannot glory in anything that would limit our creatureliness to being a child of the world or in anything that would substitute itself for God, who alone can be God.

Glory in God

And yet we are to glory. God has created us for glory. He has made us for a proper boasting, a proper trust, and a proper hope. The prophet says: "Let him who glories glory in this, that he understands and knows Me, that I am the Lord who practice kindness, justice, and righteousness in the earth; for in these things I delight, says the Lord." Here is something to boast of. We know God. We know God, who has given Himself in relationship to us. Our knowing of Him is not to be simply a knowing about Him. We know Him in the sense that our lives are intimately bound up with Him. We are drawn up into His life by what He practices in our lives for us. In Him our lives are not limited to a narrow base which the self has created out of wisdom or might or riches. In Him our lives are extended beyond mere existence in the world of sense and smell, of feeling and frailty. In Him we transcend the world by what He does for us and in us.

He is the God who practices kindness and justice and righteousness in the earth. He practices kindness. The Hebrew word *chesedh* more literally means "faithfulness." He practices kindness because of His faithfulness to the covenant which He has made with His people. This means that even when they rebelled or displayed their weakness and deserved His judgment and condemnation, God in His mercy would deal with them on the basis of the covenant. He would still be their God, and they would be His people.

We experience this faithfulness of God in the manner in which He deals with us through our Lord Jesus Christ. Though we are deserving of our own fate, death, in Jesus Christ God willingly sets aside our sin. There is something to glory in. By God's faithfulness to His covenant, by His practice of kindness we are translated from the kingdom of this world into the kingdom of His grace, lifted out from under condemnation and placed in the order of His salvation. By faith, by knowing this God, we become the creatures we were intended to be, and by faith we know that our God is a God who practices kindness in the earth.

If we are to glory in God, we must know, too, that He practices justice in the earth. The Hebrew word *mishpat,* "justice," means not a justice that is administered by the Law alone, a justice that would condemn and kill. This justice is administered in the light of the covenant. This means that, to be sure, the Law must damn man for his sin, must put him under death and the threat of hell. When man fails to trust God's mercy, then this would be his final judgment. However, justice administered by the covenant also means that by virtue of God's own testimony, in view of His own promise, and on the basis of what God had done for His people, He must set aside the sin of those who trust Him and would repent of their sin. There is something to glory in.

We who know this God in Jesus Christ know that He is a God of great justice. We know that He is our Judge. But we also know that He has established a covenant and sealed the covenant with the blood of His Son Jesus, by which He can set aside His judgment of our sins.

But more than that. This God also practices righteousness in the earth. Now how can a God practice righteousness in the earth when all His creatures are sinners? The answer is found in the real glory of the covenant relationship. God was willing to call this sinful people of Israel His people, a holy people. Not only does this holy and righteous God set aside their sins, but He also gives them righteousness, He imputes it to them.

We now know that He gives us His own righteousness in Christ Jesus. What belongs to Jesus Christ He makes ours in faith. He makes us His own in Jesus Christ; in that Christ He makes us like unto Himself. He makes us new creatures. And what God gives us in Christ will never fail us. When we glory in what He has done for us in Jesus Christ, we glory in that which will not fade away. Death has no threat against this work which God has begun in us.

Let us then not glory in anything other than this. When we are tempted to glory in something other than the God of our Lord Jesus Christ, remember that that glory will soon pass and we would die with it. Rather let us glory in this, that we know the one and only true God, "who practices kindness, justice, and righteousness in the earth" through our Lord Jesus Christ.

Who Will Find a Word from the Lord?

"Behold, the days are coming," says the Lord God, "when I will send a famine on the land; not a famine of bread, nor a thirst for water, but of hearing the words of the Lord. They shall wander from sea to sea and from north to east; they shall run to and fro to seek the Word of the Lord, but they shall not find it."

Amos 8:11, 12 (RSV)

ᴥᏸ *Who Will Find a Word from the Lord?* ᏸᴥ

A MOS, the shepherd of Tekoa, is representative of the manner in which the Old Testament prophets were awakened to their calling. Coming out of the wilderness to peaceful, prosperous, and plush Israel, Amos was rankled by the callous indifference to God's Word. It was not because the people did not practice religion. On the contrary they were diligent in making their sacrifices and sustaining the religious life. What disturbed Amos was that the people were too comfortable in their religion. They had glossed over their sins of social injustices and sanctified their quiet prosperity as God's good pleasure with them.

What Amos had to say to this people is a word that must be spoken to any people which believes that its religiosity is in itself a guarantee of its peace. The prophetic proclamation of Amos is a fitting word in this day when people are apt to appraise the international situation in terms of godless nation versus a godly nation. The assumption appears to be that the nation that does not speak out against religion will have the blessing of Almighty God. Amos would make it quite clear that the situation is far more complicated than this. To the prophet the call of religion was to be more than religious; to him religion was the call to be faithful to the God who rules all things. It was the call to trust the Word of the Lord. What we need to learn of this prophet is that we can find no security in what we are saying about God but that security rests only in our obedience to what God says to us.

Where Is a Word of the Lord?

But you immediately raise the question, Who will find a word of the Lord among the many words which we hear about God? There is a saturation of words about God. There is an infinite variety of interpretations of words which are supposedly words from God or inspired words about Him. There are numerous world religions and an endless variety of sects, denominations, and cults within each of them. The average layman suffers from a satiety of words that have been preached at him from all corners. And you might probably argue that it may have been no different in the day of Amos. How could the ordinary people determine for themselves what was a word from God? The priests and the organized religion were saying one thing, and Amos was saying another. How could the people make the decision? And what about our situation today? The theologians appear to be pitted against one another. We hear about the language about religion and the language of religion, the language about faith and the language of faith, the language against faith and the language in defense of the faith. How are we to make the judgment? That is a fair question and deserving of an answer.

However, before we attempt the answer to the question, we should note that the prophet was not unaware of what he was doing. He was highly conscious of what his prophetic task was. He was not indifferent to the fact that he openly opposed the priests and the organized religion. He knew that he was creating consternation among the people. And yet he was confident that it was his task and his calling to make the radical demand that people listen for the word from God through him. He had the audacity to tell this people, which drew all of their national sentiment and character from their cultic religion, that they would experience a famine of hearing the words of the Lord in their land unless they listened to him.

History proved Amos right. In spite of their cultic observances and the religious words, the Word of the Lord was eclipsed in this land, and the people came to their destruction. And the situation has been repeated often among the people of the earth who believed that they were God's children and possessed proper words about Him. The medieval church was extensive and had every appearance of being religious, and yet we know that there was a "famine of hearing the words of the Lord." Germany, the cradle of the Reformation, once boasted a proper loyalty to the heavenly Father, but that nation has been rocked many times by great upheaval and even now may know something of a "famine of hearing the words of the Lord."

And how about our own nation? Will Herberg's study *Protestant — Catholic — Jew* has had a wide reading. The thesis of Herberg's book is that the third-generation Americans are seeking identity through organized religion. Yet that appears to be all they seek for the most part. There is little genuine religious conviction, and religious affiliations are to a great degree purely sociological. The theme of many current novels is that man in search of great religious experience may have to find it outside organized religion. That may be a valid observation. There can readily be a "famine of hearing the words of the Lord" where one would least expect it. Yet we should not be surprised. Is not this the truth of the common parable which our Lord speaks in the holy Gospel for today about the sower and the soils?

The Word may be sown, but the soils will not bring forth fruit simply because the seed has fallen on them. The Word has to take root in the heart.

So we can find no easy refuge from the Word which the prophet Amos addresses to us. We cannot excuse ourselves because there are many words about God. He warns us lest we put ourselves into the dilemma of not being able to find a word from God, because it will be hidden from us. But why should it be hidden from us when it was so obvious to him?

The Word Is Open to the Prophet

The word from the Lord was not hidden to Amos at all. To Amos the Word of the Lord was an open word. God's Word was His action. God is sovereign and transcendent, a God above all things and over all things. Yet He is the God in nature and the God in history. His action can be seen both in nature and in history. Amos could read God's judgment in the plague of locusts that devoured the fruit of the field. If the fruit of the field is so devoured, what would keep Israel from being destroyed? If the fire devoured the land, what would prevent Israel from a judgment by fire? And if a dead, inanimate wall had to be placed under the judgment of the mason's plumbline, what exempted Israel from the plumbline of God's judgments? And if the basket of summer fruit is the sign that fall is come and that the death of winter will soon arrive, Israel could know that her prosperity would wither and that her fall was inevitable.

So homely were the visions of God's judgment which Amos saw for his people, but they were the actions of God which were open to all. They were words which God spoke clearly in all that surrounded this people. They were visions which all men could see if they would open their eyes to see that God is in their situations. They were words that all men could hear if they would open their ears to permit God to speak to them.

But Amos also recalled God's action in history for His people. He recalled for them the exodus, when He brought this people out of the land of Egypt. He remembered how God raised up for them prophets to speak His Word to them. It is this God who gave them such evidence of His love and His mercy: a God who continued to act for this people, who tried to correct them, who gave further evidence of His love to them that they should hear and trust. This was the God this people had offended and forsaken. He had spoken clearly to them in their history, and He was speaking to them again through the prophet in clear and unmistakable terms. "The Lord roars from Zion and utters His voice from Jerusalem" (1:2). For Amos this Word was a sustained plea for the people to repent and worship again the God who disclosed Himself in mercy to them. The Word he preached demanded obedience to this God lest destruction come upon them. It is interesting to note that the book offers no hope of restoration except for the last chapter, which is believed to be the addition of preachers after Amos who again referred to the exodus as the assurance of God's faithfulness to His people.

For us this Word should have the same kind of cutting edge. God has not changed in the manner of His dealing with men. God still rules in history and in the creation. We must be mindful of the terrible doom that befalls us when we neglect the revelation of God's grace in Christ. Amos preached doom for Israel, and doomed she was. Annihilation beset her. In our day we need not elaborate on the destruction that can befall us. Should it befall us, it would be because we neglect this Word given to us in this age of grace. And what excuse would we have? Are we going to try to blame God for not being more clear in His demands, His judgments, or His grace?

As Amos called the people back to what God had disclosed in history, God calls us back to what He has disclosed in the Lord Jesus Christ, in whom He delivered us from the bondage to the world of judgment and death. In Christ He ushers us into the rule of His grace and His love. By the death and resurrection of the Lord Jesus Christ He has signed to us His faithful and saving intentions for us. It is in Christ then that we can read, learn, and hear His Word. It is in Christ then that we can become obedient unto Him. It is in Christ that we can trust Him. It is in Christ that we learn what we can expect of Him. It is in Christ that we discover what the future can hold for us. It is in Christ that there can never be a "famine of hearing the words of the Lord." And because of this Christ, you and I find ourselves without excuse.

Do we look for what to believe? Do we wonder what we should believe? Do we search for some touchstone by which we can judge what is essential to believing? Jesus Christ is our Answer. What God has revealed in Him about His grace and His love for us is what is essential to our lives. We can measure the doctrine, the preaching, the behavior, the action of the church on the basis of this one thing, that God has made Himself Father through Christ.

There is no need to wander to and fro in the land, to go from east to west looking for a word from the Lord. Christ is the Center of all. He is the East and the West. All things are gathered up into Him. Let us trust that Word which God has made Him to be, and let us be obedient unto Him,

A Time to Return

◄§ *You shall say to them, Thus says the Lord: When men fall, do they not rise again? If one turns away, does he not return? Why then has this people turned away in perpetual backsliding? They hold fast to deceit, they refuse to return. I have given heed and listened, but they have not spoken aright; no man repents of his wickedness, saying, "What have I done?" Everyone turns to his own course like a horse plunging headlong into battle. Even the stork in the heavens knows her times; and the turtledove, swallow, and crane keep the time of their coming; but My people know not the ordinance of the Lord. How can you say, "We are wise, and the Law of the Lord is with us"? But behold, the false pen of the scribes has made it into a lie. The wise men shall be put to shame, they shall be dismayed and taken; lo, they have rejected the Word of the Lord, and what wisdom is in them?* §►

Jeremiah 8:4-9 (RSV)

⊸§ A Time to Return §⊱

THE most often repeated charge against a religion of grace is that it is too easy. All one need do is make confession of his sin, receive pardon, and return to his former way of life. Such a superficial criticism of the Gospel fails to reckon with deep-seated difficulty which people have in making confession.

Some years ago two gentlemen of the community made a serious charge against one of the members of my congregation. They requested that I speak to the man. If he made confession and was willing to amend, they would drop the matter. If not, they would speak to him in my presence. If he refused to confess to them, they would take the matter to a court of law. I met with the accused, explained that a serious charge had been made against him. I was not in position to make a judgment in the matter but desired to help. The accused did not confess before me or his accusers. Eventually, in a court of law, he confessed his guilt and was sentenced to prison.

The problem for this man was that he did not know or understand the proper time for confession. He did not know a good time to return to an accurate accounting of himself.

Unrepentance Is Unnatural

The problem of confession before God or man is not uncommon. The prophet Jeremiah was sensitive to the problem in his day. He revealed that God's patience with man's unwillingness to repent was sorely tried. What is to be noted about this unyielding, unrelenting attitude of man toward his sin is that it is unnatural from God's point of view. This is the burden of Jeremiah's proclamation.

Man's unrepentant attitude is unnatural when compared with man's ability to recover from other setbacks. Jeremiah proclaims that God asks: "When men fall, do they not rise again? If one turns away, does he not return?" This is the natural reaction one expects. When our nation put its first astronaut into orbit around the globe, much attention was given to the fact that this was America's return to the space race. The downfallen spirits about another nation's achievements were now elevated by this success. The world of sports knows this kind of return too. When the ballplayer in the major leagues goes down to the minors, the fans cheer him on if he makes it back to the majors. We herald this kind of story as triumph of the human spirit. Business showers its accolades, too, on the enterprising spirit that weathers the storms of bust and depression to make it back into the ranks of competitors. We count it natural that the man who is down does not want to remain down but that he draws on all his resources to get back to his previous position.

It is not so with man in his sin. Jeremiah reports that God complains: "Why then has this people turned away in perpetual backsliding? They hold fast to deceit, they refuse to return. I have given heed and listened, but they have not spoken aright; no man repents of his wickedness, saying, 'What have I done?' Everyone turns to his own course like a horse plunging headlong into battle." Whereas man may bounce back from his setbacks in his daily routine, he is an

utter failure at sizing up his inner failings. He appears unwilling to admit he is steadily falling farther from his God.
He is not the man that he should be, and really he knows it.
But he does nothing about it. He falls deeper and deeper
into this condition. He slides back farther and farther. He
creates a wider gulf between himself and his Maker.

A man may cover for this condition by "holding fast to
deceit." He may permit himself to be deluded into believing
that everything is all right between himself and God. He
may think of himself as being righteous and acceptable and
good by the standards which he himself has set. Usually
this standard is his fellowman, whom he struggles to outdo
in his behavior. But that is rank deceit because it hides
the real issue. A man cannot know his true self by com-
paring himself with his fellow creature. He can know the
true self only when he compares himself with his Creator.
Consequently such a man "refuses to return." He is as far
off base as he can be, and he doesn't know it.

But God listens and waits. He waits for the man to
awaken to the reality of condition. He waits for him to
"repent of his wickedness" and to say, "What have I done?"
God's waiting appears to be in vain. In Jeremiah's day, as
well as in our own, the true confession of man's plight is
missing. Even in our own day, when the admission of man's
meaninglessness and his lack of purpose is so open, when
men are so pessimistic about man, men still fail to admit
that they are alienated from God. They would still deceive
themselves about that point.

Regardless of whether men are optimistic about themselves or whether they are pessimistic, if they fail to return
to God in confession before Him, they seal their own doom.
Following "his own course," each is "like a horse plunging

headlong into battle." A war horse is a noble animal, but without a rider to guide him and lead him he is certain to make the death plunge or be captured by the enemy. He serves no purpose in the battle except to add to the confusion of the day, to thicken the traffic of death, and to heighten the disaster. The man who has failed to return to his Creator is no different. He adds to the confusions of life, he clutters the empty strivings of man with more meaninglessness, and he rushes headlong on to his doom-filled death.

Jeremiah reports that God notices that the birds of the air fare better than man. "Even the stork in the heavens knows her times; and the turtledove, swallow, and crane keep the time of their coming; but My people know not the ordinance of the Lord." The winged creatures obey the laws of nature which God has created. They make their flights to warmer climes when winter sets in, and they return on schedule for the spring. By the natural instincts which God has given them they obey Him and fulfill the purposes for which He created them. But not so man. He refuses to obey the ordinances of God. His natural instincts are so warped, his sin so unnatural that he does not have enough sense to return to his God. The dumb fowl chirp eloquent sermons to man as they return in their flight, but man in his natural condition is so unnatural that he does not pay heed. He remains unyielding and unrelenting. He remains in his sin.

Repentance Comes Through a Death

The second part of our text is the beginning of a new stanza in Jeremiah's proclamation. It starts a new thought but is not totally unrelated to the foregoing. The people who have the Law are not necessarily repentant either.

"How can you say, 'We are wise, and the Law of the Lord is with us'? But behold, the false pen of the scribes has made it into a lie. The wise men shall be put to shame, they shall be dismayed and taken; lo, they have rejected the Word of the Lord, and what wisdom is in them?"

Even those who handled the very Law of the Lord had not become wise. They had mishandled the Word. The scribes had been ever so careful to transmit the Word of the Law in its purity. They had been diligent in their attempt to explicate the Word in such a way that they could say, "The Law of the Lord is with us. We have it. We know what it says, we know what it means, and we are living according to it. Therefore God is with us." But God says they have falsified the Word of the Torah, the Scripture. They have made it a dead thing. They have emptied the Word of its significance and meaning. In their hands it is no longer the Word of God. They had changed the Word of God into a lie. By their use of the Word they did not need to repent and they did not need to obey. They were obedient unto a dead word which they could manipulate to their good pleasure and say, "The Torah of the Lord is with us." They refused to listen to the Word of God as it came to them through the prophet. They came neither to repentance nor to faith, because they would not heed the living Word from the mouth of one whom God had sent.

What the unrepentant did in Jeremiah's day and what they continue to do in our day is made clearer for us in the holy Gospel for today. Jesus said to the Twelve: "Behold, we are going up to Jerusalem, and everything that is written of the Son of Man by the prophets will be accomplished. For He will be delivered to the Gentiles and will be mocked and shamefully treated and spit upon; they will scourge

Him and kill Him, and on the third day He will rise" (Luke 18:31-33). On the one hand, no better illustration of the resistance of unrepentant man is given than in the crucifixion of our Lord. Unrepentant men crucified our Lord, and they crucify Him anew by their continued unrepentance. On the other hand, no better illustration of obedience to the Word of the Lord is given than in the life of our Lord. He went up to Jerusalem knowing full well all that was involved in His appearance there.

When Jesus went up to Jerusalem, He was fully conscious that the continued resistance of those who did not accept His ministry of grace as One sent by God could end only in His death. Yet He went. He knew, too, that by their misuse of the Law He could be condemned to death. Yet He went. He had been placed under the Law by the heavenly Father, and being obedient unto the Father, He would die under the Law. But He was also confident, full of trust and faith that the Father would raise Him from the dead. And so He went, obedient to the Father under the Law, full of faith in the Father's promise.

In the Christ, in His journey to Jerusalem we learn how to be obedient to the Law and full of faith in God's promise. In this journey we see what is involved in making confession under the Law. The Word calls us to make the journey with Him. Under the Law, we, too, must be slain. The old man, the old life of sin, the former life of alienation must be put to death in Christ. In our confession we acknowledge that the Christ who dies on a cross should be ourselves. As we see this Christ on a cross, we go to our knees and ask what God wants to hear: "What have I done?" And then we pour out before Him all that we have done wrong in our unfaith and our unbelief. We confess all that has been the basis of our false pride, our false gods, and our false hopes. Before this Christ we know what it is to return and to confess. If we have not learned it from the man who returns from his setback, if we have not learned it from the riderless warhorse, if we have not learned it from the birds, if we have not learned it from the words of the Law, then let us learn it here. For this Christ on the cross is God's last and best Word to us to call us to repentance. And if we cannot learn it here, then where will we learn it?

But if we learn repentance at this cross, we also may hear what it is that God would say to us when we repent. For God desires that we repent only that He may speak a word of grace, forgiveness, and life to us. He yearns for us to return that He may restore us to our former position as His children and heirs of His eternity. He raised Christ from the dead. And in raising Christ from the dead He gave promise to all who would trust Him. He gave promise to all who, slain by His Law in their repentance, would trust that He will remain faithful unto them. This living Christ is God's living Word to you and to me; to Him we are called to be faithful.

Is the Christian religion easy? Yes! Yes, for him who dies with Christ in daily confession of his sin that God might daily raise him in Christ.

Let us then return to our God by going up to Jerusalem with Him.

⤳ *Now the serpent was more subtle than any other wild creature that the Lord God had made. He said to the woman, "Did God say, 'You shall not eat of any tree of the garden'?" And the woman said to the serpent, "We may eat of the fruit of the trees of the garden; but God said, 'You shall not eat of the fruit of the tree which is in the midst of the garden, neither shall you touch it, lest you die.' " But the serpent said to the woman, "You will not die. For God knows that when you eat of it your eyes will be opened, and you will be like God, knowing good and evil." So when the woman saw that the tree was good for food and that it was a delight to the eyes and that the tree was to be desired to make one wise, she took of its fruit and ate; and she also gave some to her husband, and he ate. Then the eyes of both were opened, and they knew that they were naked; and they sewed fig leaves together and made themselves aprons. And they heard the sound of the Lord God walking in the garden in the cool of the day, and the man and his wife hid themselves from the presence of the Lord God among the trees of the garden. But the Lord God called to the man and said to him, "Where are you?" And he said, "I heard the sound of Thee in the garden, and I was afraid because I was naked; and I hid myself." He said, "Who told you that you were naked? Have you eaten of the tree of which I commanded you not to eat?" The man said, "The woman whom Thou gavest to be with me, she gave me fruit of the tree, and I ate." Then the Lord God said to the woman, "What is this that you have done?" The woman said, "The serpent beguiled me, and I ate." The Lord God said to the serpent, "Because you have done this, cursed are you above all cattle and above all wild animals; upon your belly you shall go, and dust you shall eat all the days of your life. I will put enmity between you and the woman and between your seed and her Seed; He shall bruise your head, and you shall bruise His heel."* ક➤

Genesis 3:1-15 (RSV)

❧ *Temptation* ❧

THE first American astronaut to go into orbit reported breathtaking views of our planet, its sunrises, sunsets, and the stillness of its nights. Perhaps it is with a proper kind of envy that we long to share a view comparable to that of the primeval day when the Creator looked at the creation and saw that it was good. Or we long for the feeling of weightlessness, to be released from the harnesses of this creation, not simply its own gravity but the gravity of our sin and our guilt.

Yet all the lure and wonder of the space age is darkened by the shadow of our doubt. We have good reason to worry if we can leave space inviolate, if we can leave it uncontaminated by the virus of our sin. The history of man tragically reveals that nowhere and at no time has he passed over into new boundaries without his sin and his temptations to haunt him. He has blazed trails to new worlds, new frontiers, new lands, and new cities, but nowhere has he been able to insulate himself against the temptations which have victimized him.

Temptation to Unbelief

Why must men lose out to temptation? Why are we so easily snared by the cunning of the powers of darkness?

The answer is clearly revealed in Adam's fall. Here we have the account of how Satan makes his thrust, uncovers our weakness, and makes us his subjects. The temptations come to us as they did to Eve, disguised in subtleties, friendliness, and even godliness. None of us is likely to desire to be tempted or to be ungodlike, and our temptations are rarely that bold and that pronounced. Instead the temptation eases itself in on us at the point where we are the most susceptible. The serpent says to the woman, "Did God say, 'You shall not eat of any tree of the garden'?" That's the place for the temptation to begin. Cast doubt on the Word of God. Put the Word under a shadow. Doesn't that have a familiar ring for you? How many times has not your heart been filled with this uncertainty? Is God really reliable and trustworthy in the Word? Or could God possibly mean it when He says I should be willing to share my little fortunes so that the church can minister to people in far-off Hong Kong? Could God really mean it when He commands me to be chaste and decent in the sex life? Really, is not that taking oneself too seriously? What good could my little contribution possibly do among the hungry multitudes in Hong Kong, and isn't one also expected to take care of oneself? And isn't the command for sexual purity out of date for our time and our society? Besides, didn't God give us these sex drives in the first place?

Once such doubt in God's truthfulness is established, then unbelief replaces faith and trust quite handily. Doubt in the hand of the Tempter is the broom to sweep away confidence in God and His ways. When the woman registers the beginnings of her doubt, "God said, 'You shall not eat of the fruit of the tree which is in the midst of the garden, neither shall you touch it, lest you die,'" she had already altered the word from God, "You shall surely die." The serpent picks up this doubt and builds on it: "You will not die. For God knows that when you eat of it your eyes will be opened, and you will be like God, knowing good and evil." Once the doubt has been established, its conversion to unbelief is mastered by a bold stroke.

You and I have experienced this over and over again in our own lives. Once we get into this position of doubting the relevance and importance of God's Word for our situation, most generally we have succumbed to the temptation. Helmut Thielecke has properly pointed out that there is little value in prayer once the temptation has reached this stage. Our Lord properly does not teach us in the Lord's Prayer to pray, "Help us in our temptation," but, "Lead us not into temptation." We are to pray that by God's grace He might keep us away, separated from the temptation, for the doubt of His grace and promise too readily blurs into unbelief.

So it happened for Eve. She "saw that the tree was good for food and that it was a delight to the eyes and that the tree was desired to make one wise," and she took and ate. Luther noted from the description of Eve's sin that it is characteristic of our sin that while we are actively engaged by the sin there is no sense of guilt. Whether thinking, doing, performing, talking — whatever the activity may be — there is no sense of sin, for the deeper sin of unbelief has already taken place. The outward act, however, engages the whole man and perverts his whole being. With her ears Eve had listened to the Tempter's lie. With her eyes she had examined the tree and its fruits. With her hands she reached and plucked the fruit, which was pleasant to smell and taste. The serpent had not tried to make her his victim by appealing to these things. He has confined himself to making God a liar. And once this lie established itself in the heart and mind of Eve, she surrendered her whole being to the lie. And when she and Adam ate of the fruit, their sin permeated their whole being in the same way that the fruit stuck to their ribs.

Immediately "the eyes of both were opened, and they knew that they were naked; and they sewed fig leaves together and made themselves aprons . . . and they hid themselves from the presence of the Lord." So man's sin comes to haunt him. The sin was the sin of unbelief. Man had given himself to a lie. God had created man in His own image. Man was given the faculties to think, to choose, to decide. He was capable of a relationship with his Creator. He had the power of communication. But above all, he transcended the creation. He was above the creation, dependent on God for His being, not dependent on the creation. He was a ruler of the creation, not to be ruled by it. He was like God in this image. Adam and Eve's sin was that they failed to believe it. Their sin was that they failed to believe that God had been faithful and true to them. They were no longer above the creation. They had enslaved themselves to it. Their sin so perverted their minds and their hearts that they could not believe that God was still their God. They could not stand His presence. They had to hide themselves, hide their guilt behind clothing of leaves and hide themselves in the forests of the creation.

Thus it is that we in our unfaith know this perversity of the whole being. In our sin of unbelief, or our sins which all flow from unbelief, we cannot stand in the presence of the holy God, but we dodge and hide away from Him. It is this running from Him that leaves us with a sense of rootlessness, emptiness, and futility. And should we keep running, we should be cut off from Him completely. We should be left to die alone the death that Adam ushered in by his sin and which we die by reason of our sin.

God Destroys the Power of Temptation

However, God does not leave the sinner alone. He seeks him out. He searches for him. He invades his haunts, his places of hiding, the forests of his guilt. Luther says that when God came to Adam and Eve, He came in gentleness, kindliness, and fatherliness. He does not come to drive Adam away from Himself. God puts Adam on trial by asking, "Where are you?" But this is for the purpose of bringing Adam to a sense of his sin. He wants to call Adam back from his sin. It is Adam who has condemned himself. He is afraid of God's presence by reason of his sin. Caught in his sin, he tries to escape by transferring his guilt to God. But God would speak a gracious word to Adam to demonstrate that He has not changed in His faithfulness. Even when He speaks the Law to Adam, He is a gracious Father who would draw His child to Himself. He desires to enter into the human situation to do battle with the forces that have now engulfed man. He gives promise that He will engage Himself in the conflict that was the inevitable result of the Fall. "I will put enmity between you [the serpent] and the woman and between your seed and her Seed; He shall bruise your head, and you shall bruise His heel."

This gracious promise becomes incarnate in the holy Gospel for today. The Lord Jesus Christ, whom Paul calls the Second Adam, is tempted of Satan in the same manner as was the first Adam. The temptation is the same. It is a temptation about food. Hunger becomes the occasion for doubting the ways of God. It is a temptation to distrust

134

God. "If you are the Son of God, command these stones to become loaves of bread" (Matt. 4:3). Jesus is the Son of God. To yield to this temptation would be to distrust that He is, to lose confidence in God as the Father, to destroy the relationship with the Father, who cares for His Son in His hungry state. This temptation was to be repeated over and over again in the life of our Lord until He finally comes to the cross. Even there He is tempted again: "If You are the Son of God, come down from the cross." (Matt. 27:40)

But the Christ refused to be drawn into the temptation. As He stated at the first temptation: "Man shall not live by bread alone but by every word that proceeds from the mouth of God" (Matt. 4:4). He trusted and relied on the promises which the Father had given Him. He did not lose His confidence in God. He trusted Him even in death. And when God raised the Christ from the dead, He thereby indicated that in all that the Lord Jesus had done He was the Mediator of our salvation. His refusal to yield to the temptation of the devil, His perfect trust and obedience to the Father under the Law, His perfect trust in death was the crushing of the serpent's head. He had been bruised in the death which the serpent had brought to the world, but He was victorious in death and brought back life from the tomb.

The apostle Paul writes that the effect of the work of the Lord Jesus is to offer life to all: "As one man's trespass led to condemnation for all men, so one Man's act of righteousness leads to acquittal and life for all men. For as by one man's disobedience many were made sinners, so by one Man's obedience many will be made righteous" (Rom. 5:18, 19). The Christ comes to deliver us from our disobedience. In Him we are restored to relationship with the heavenly Father. He is God's Promise to us, fulfilled and realized, so that now we may live in Him by hope.

Christ is our Answer to temptation. In Christ we see that the devil is a liar. In Christ we see that Adam was wrong. In Christ we see that we are wrong when we doubt for one moment God's goodness and grace. In Christ we see that we are become the children of God once more by reason of the forgiveness which He grants us. In Christ we see that we need not doubt this for one moment. There is no need to prove it but only to trust it.

And do you not see what it is that our Lord has prepared for us in His Holy Supper? It is here that He calls us to taste of His righteousness. In Adam and like Adam we have yielded ourselves completely to the fruit of unfaith, which is sin. In this sacrament our Lord gives us His true body and blood and the fruit of His supreme sacrifice, of His vicarious atonement: the forgiveness of sins, His holiness and righteousness, and everlasting life in heaven. And as sin stuck to man to bring death, so the Lord's Supper strengthens our faith, our spiritual life, and enables us to lead a holier life, filled with the hope of the resurrection. With the bread and wine in the sacrament the Lord Jesus gives us Himself, His body and blood, given and shed for us for the remission of sins. Thus "God shows His love for us in that, while we were yet sinners, Christ died for us."

This then is our confidence in the face of temptation. We know that God would guard and keep us so that the devil, the world, and our flesh may not deceive us or mislead us into unbelief, despair, and other great and shameful sins, but that, although we may be so tempted, we may finally prevail and gain the victory. (Sixth Petition, Luther's Small Catechism)

The People of God

☙ Moses said to the Lord, "See, Thou sayest to me, 'Bring up this people'; but Thou hast not let me know whom Thou wilt send with me. Yet Thou hast said, 'I know you by name, and you have also found favor in My sight.' Now therefore, I pray Thee, if I have found favor in Thy sight, show me now Thy ways that I may know Thee and find favor in Thy sight. Consider too that this nation is Thy people." And He said, "My presence will go with you, and I will give you rest." And he said to Him, "If Thy presence will not go with me, do not carry us up from here. For how shall it be known that I have found favor in Thy sight, I and Thy people? Is it not in Thy going with us so that we are distinct, I and Thy people, from all other people that are upon the face of the earth?" ☙

Exodus 33:12-16 (RSV)

◦⋗ *The People of God* ⋖◦

THE present moment of history brings again into sharp focus the inability of men to live together. Our own nation builds ghettoes with racial prejudices. The rise of independent nations has stirred nationalism on the great continents of Africa and Asia. A wall in Berlin has become the symbol of the division between East and West. But this is not new. Men are keeping alive the artificial separations that divide them. They have concretized their differences. They have made systems out of their differences. They have devised separate political, economic, and social systems that make them appear hopelessly incompatible. They also have used religion to sanction their systems that they might appear as a people of God.

But to be a people of God is not to be nationalistic. The people of God transcends the boundaries of nationalism. The ancient people of God, holy Israel, was no nation in the ordinary sense. Israel was the people of God in a special and unique way. And in this uneasy day when men again would have us identify nationalism with religion, or religion with nationalism, when they would sanction their causes with the name of God, it is good to remember what it means to be the people of God.

The People of God Live Under a Covenant

For ancient Israel to be a people of God meant to stand under a covenant with God. When Israel had been delivered from Egypt in the exodus, by faith they knew that God would be their God and they His people. To the prophet Moses had come the revelation that God would bind Himself to this people by a covenant, a pledge, and a promise, and the people would bind themselves to God by faith and obedience.

However, the story relates that when Moses ascended into the mount to receive the revelation which was given him, the people became impatient during the 40 days. They switched their allegiance from the God of Israel to an idol. This idolatry and apostasy angered God and infuriated Moses. Moses returns from the mount to punish the people. But he returns to the mount as an intercessor and a mediator for his people. Yet it appears that the matter is settled in the mind of God: "Depart, go up hence, you and the people whom you have brought up out of the land of Egypt, to the land of which I swore to Abraham, Isaac, and Jacob, saying, 'To your descendants I will give it.' . . . But I will not go up among you lest I consume you in the way, for you are a stiff-necked people."

God had been benevolent, faithful, and gracious in His intentions for this people. But clearly they had rejected Him. He would keep the outer promise. He would deliver them to the land He had promised. However, He could not promise His presence. They had made the promise of His presence impossible by their unbelief. For Him to be present among such a rebellious people would invite their immediate judgment and destruction. Far better they should go alone. There perhaps, without His presence in the promise, they would come to difficulty and distress. Perhaps in a future day of trouble they would remember His promise and invite His gracious presence once again.

So God must always deal with us in our rebellion. He yearns to serve us by His good grace and love, but we spurn His offers over and over again. We count His love and forgiveness as unimportant and replace Him with cheap gods of gold and pleasure. And when we do, we have to withdraw ourselves from His presence in the promise. He is with us only in an outward way, waiting for us to trip and stumble in the days of trouble we ourselves create. He waits, hoping that we will return to His gracious promises and invite His presence anew.

Moses did recall the promise of God. He remembered the covenant. He is startled to think that God would not dwell with His people in the manner He has dwelt with them to this moment. He refuses to budge from this place unless God will attend Israel. The command which God has given him is utterly meaningless if God will not attend His people. "See, Thou sayest to me, 'Bring up this people'; but Thou hast not let me know whom Thou wilt send with me." For what possible purpose could God send this people up to possess a new land if He is not present with them? Neither God's command nor the people's response to it would be significant without the presence of God.

Life is always meaningless for us without the gracious promises of God. His presence is essential to life. What good does it do us to live our days if we have no purpose for living? In what way can we find purpose unless the God who created us gives us the purpose? By what stretch of the imagination can we hope to explore the meaning of life unless our Creator gives us some clue? What good is life, what good is any activity of life, what good are any heroics or adventures of life if our God should abandon us in the midst of life?

"No," says Moses, "do not abandon us now. Strike us dead here and now if Thou art not gracious toward us. But don't force us into any kind of struggle of life, don't ask anything of us, don't push us on unless Thou wilt attend us. Life is nothing without Thee. It is death. What good will it do to possess a land of milk and honey if we cannot possess Thee? Why prolong our misery? Why postpone our death? It would be better to die now." This is the sense of Moses' thought. He does not let the matter rest here. He appeals to the covenant: "Yet Thou hast said, 'I know you by name, and you have also found favor in My sight.' Now therefore, I pray Thee, if I have found favor in Thy sight, show me now Thy ways that I may know Thee and find favor in Thy sight. Consider too that this nation is Thy people."

Moses remembers that God had disclosed that He is a gracious God. He knew Moses by name. In His grace He granted great favor to this man and his people. He had cared for them once. He had loved them, saved them, and redeemed them from bondage. Furthermore, this was His people. He had created them. How could He abandon them? "Show me Thy ways," says Moses. Moses is an obedient and faithful servant. He is a true mediator. When all others have been disobedient, rebellious, unfaithful, he alone stands before God in faith, trust, and obedience, pressing God to remember His promise, to show His mercy and love to this people, which is His people. In this role Moses prefigures our blessed Lord Jesus Christ, who by His perfect obedience and holy faith stood alone as our Mediator in the world of unfaithfulness. As mediator, Moses, like Christ who came after him, reminds us that the people of God stand under the covenant, the promise, and they may appeal by faith to God's grace at all times.

God Abides by His Covenant with His People

God acquiesced to the pleadings of Moses. "My presence will go with you, and I will give you rest." There is no argument against the case which Moses states. There is no rebuttal. There is no attempt to justify a harsh treatment of this people. There is no further word about abandonment. Moses is right. God is a faithful God. He is gracious and good. But He cannot be gracious if none would let Him be gracious. He cannot be good if men will close their eyes and their hearts to His goodness. By the faith of one man, Moses, God is urged to disclose His grace to this people once again. And God immediately responds with the promise of His presence. God waits for the invitation of our faith that He might come and dwell in us and among us.

Moses counts this presence of God as the distinctive and unique feature of Israel. "Is it not in Thy going with us so that we are distinct, I and Thy people, from all other people that are upon the face of the earth?" The people of God are distinct because they know this presence of God in their lives. They do not search for God, for God has come to them. They do not speculate about God, for God has disclosed His nature to them. They do not look for new words about God, for God has revealed Himself in His words, His saving actions, for them. The people of God are those with whom God dwells.

You and I understand this through our Lord Jesus Christ. In Jesus Christ God came to live and dwell with us. In Jesus Christ God gave us His presence in a unique way.

In Jesus Christ God desires us to understand that He lives in us. This is how He makes us a people of God. Jesus tells us: "The kingdom of God is not coming with signs to be observed. Nor will they say, 'Lo, here it is!' or, 'There!' For behold, the kingdom of God is in the midst of you" (Luke 17:20, 21). The same action God performed in Jesus Christ He desires to perform in you. Christ lived in firm, full, and perfect trust in God's presence. "I and the Father are one," He said (John 10:30). He did not even let death separate Him from the Father. "My God, My God, why hast Thou forsaken Me?" (Matt. 27:46). Though God was willing to abandon His Son because of the wickedness of the people, Jesus did not abandon the promise, the grace of God, and by faith still called Him "My God." On the cross He was heard to say: "Father, into Thy hands I commit My Spirit" (Luke 23:46). Therefore when God raised the Christ from the dead, He gave the solemn pledge to us all: "My presence will go with you, and I will give you rest." In the Christ God gives us assurance that even in death He will attend us and bring us into the eternal rest.

In the holy Gospel for today we hear a story which elucidates what it means to be the people of God. The Savior and His disciples are in the region of Tyre and Sidon, where they are disturbed by the pleading of a Canaanite woman. This is clearly outside the regions of the Jewish boundaries, and this woman quite obviously is not of the Hebrew faith. In fact she was considered to be a heathen, and the disciples are embarrassed by her presence. The disciples request that Jesus do something to get rid of her. Our Lord indicates that He has come to save the lost sheep of the house of Israel. She makes a further plea for help. He answers that it is not good to take the children's bread and throw it to dogs. In effect He says: "You are not of the people of God. You are not even a people. You are as dogs." She replies, "Even the dogs eat the crumbs that fall from their master's table." Even as a dog she had the right to assert that God is a gracious God and that He should give her at least the leftovers of His merciful promises. He commends her for her faith and grants her prayer. She had taken her place with the people of God by her faith. She trusted that God was present among His people. She refused to believe that He had not come for her. She trusted that God would not abandon her. The good and gracious God would not forsake her.

The woman of great faith is an example to us. Like Moses and our dear Lord Himself, she trusted firmly that God is a gracious God who tabernacles among us. Let that be our uniqueness. Let us not tie our faith to a flag or a race, a leftist movement or a rightist movement, the liberals or the conservatives, or any kind of ism. We have the liberty to choose by conscience what movements we will, but let us put our confidence in Him whose presence comes to us in the Christ, in His Word and in His holy sacraments. Faith in this Christ cuts through the boundaries of Tyre and Sidon, through the Berlin walls and the bamboo curtains, through time and space. For where men trust in this Christ, He is present among them to give them rest, and they are the people of God.

◄§ *In the beginning of the reign of Jehoiakim, the son of Josiah, king of Judah, this word came from the Lord: "Thus says the Lord: Stand in the court of the Lord's house, and speak to all the cities of Judah which come to worship in the house of the Lord all the words that I command you to speak to them; do not hold back a word. It may be they will listen and everyone turn from his evil way that I may repent of the evil which I intend to do to them because of their evil doings. You shall say to them, 'Thus says the Lord: If you will not listen to Me, to walk in My Law which I have set before you, and to heed the words of My servants the prophets whom I send to you urgently, though you have not heeded, then I will make this house like Shiloh, and I will make this city a curse for all the nations of the earth.' " The priests and the prophets and all the people heard Jeremiah speaking these words in the house of the Lord. And when Jeremiah had finished speaking all that the Lord had commanded him to speak to all the people, then the priests and the prophets and all the people laid hold of him, saying, "You shall die! Why have you prophesied in the name of the Lord, saying, 'This house shall be like Shiloh, and this city shall be desolate, without inhabitant'?" And all the people gathered about Jeremiah in the house of the Lord. When the princes of Judah heard these things, they came up from the king's house to the house of the Lord and took their seat in the entry of the New Gate of the house of the Lord. Then the priests and the prophets said to the princes and to all the people, "This man deserves the sentence of death because he has prophesied against this city, as you have heard with your own ears." Then Jeremiah spoke to all the princes and all the people saying, "The Lord sent me to prophesy against this house and this city all the words you have heard. Now therefore amend your ways and your doings, and obey the voice of the Lord your God, and the Lord will repent of the evil which He has pronounced against you. But as for me, behold, I am in your hands. Do with me as seems good and right to you. Only know for certain that if you put me to death, you will bring innocent blood upon yourselves and upon this city and its inhabitants, for in truth the Lord sent me to you to speak all these words in your ears."* ৽৶

Jeremiah 26:1-15 (RSV)

৺৾ *The Mark of the Prophet* ৾৹

THE periodic appearance of self-styled prophets raises the question, How would we know a prophet if one came to us? How can we tell when the preaching of the day is truly prophetic? How shall we know if the Word of God is proclaimed with true authority? We become easily impressed by the zeal of certain religious groups who come to our doors quoting Bible passages. Is their zeal a mark of the prophet? We may be encouraged by the great crowds that fill the stadia to hear a great preacher. Are the swollen statistical successes of the preacher the mark of the prophet? We may be stunned by the claims of those who call themselves faith healers. Are the case histories of healings the mark of a prophet? In the church we lay claim to keeping intact the prophetic ministry. What is the mark of that prophetic task? How can we know?

The Prophet Is Consistent with God's Revelation

In the story of Jeremiah we may look for an answer to the question. We know that Jeremiah occupies a prominent place in the prophetic history. We also know more about Jeremiah than we do about any of the other prophets. What marks him clearly as a prophet is narrated in this account. What we find here should be helpful to us in giving answer to our questions. This account is a record of how Jeremiah acquitted himself in his calling.

The most notable factor in this account is that Jeremiah speaks with the authority of God. He does not simply lay claim to this authority. He uses it. He speaks out of it. He is not guessing. He is not speculating. He speaks with assurance. He speaks with conviction. What he has to say is spoken as a "word which came from the Lord." He claims a directive from the Lord to speak this word: "Thus says the Lord: Stand in the court of the Lord's house, and speak to all the cities of Judah which come to worship in the house of the Lord all the words that I command you to speak to them."

This in itself would be little enough to commend Jeremiah as a prophet. There were other prophets who filled the precincts of Jerusalem with the same claim. That would create nothing different from the many denominational claims of our day. Baptists, Episcopalians, Lutherans, Methodists, Presbyterians, Roman Catholics, and the whole range of Christian denominations would stand and make the claim that they speak of the Word of the Lord. One could not tell from the claim alone. The claim must be substantiated by what is said.

We do not know for certain what Jeremiah did say on this occasion. Some scholars think that the temple sermon recorded in an earlier chapter was the substance of his message. It may have been this sermon which Jeremiah preached on the occasion of Jehoiakim's coronation. What we do have here is simply the outline of what he preached. What is stated here is consistent with the total production of this prophetic book. Jeremiah addresses this people concerning the wrath and the mercy of God. God would be a gracious God to this people, but if they fail to trust His mercy, He must consume them in His anger. God would be the Source of their existence and of their being, but if they refused to believe this, they were literally destroying themselves. The substance of that message is a word from the Lord.

This word of the Lord was in complete harmony with all that God had disclosed to this people in their history. This word matched everything that God had revealed through His servant Moses. This word breathed the same spirit as the prophet before him. This word was in the tradition of that great prophet Hosea, whose message greatly influenced Jeremiah. Jeremiah could review the history of his people and the action of God and could assure them of how God would spread His mercies and His grace upon them. He could appeal to the covenant and say with certainty that God would remain faithful to His people. On the other hand, Jeremiah could look upon the unfaith, the faithlessness, and the lack of trust of this people and know that they were on the brink of disaster. He could see that the religion of this people had degenerated into ritualism in the hands of the priests. This people would be sacrificed in the hands of an enemy because they did not sacrifice themselves to God. He could see that the obedience of this people had disintegrated into an outer morality and political expediency in the hands of the false prophets.

When Jeremiah looked to the growing power of Babylon — and he could see the waning spiritual power of Judah — he knew the inevitable. God would use the alien power as a servant to destroy His covenant people. When once before this people had abandoned God's covenant, God destroyed Shiloh. Shiloh had been the center of worship, the sign of God's presence among His people. Jeremiah knew therefore that God would also destroy His very own temple where He had deigned to dwell. God could not and would not live among a people who refused to acknowledge His presence in His grace. Jeremiah spoke for God. The mark of his prophetic utterance, that it was true, that it had come from God, is that it was a unity with all that God had revealed before.

The prophetic word in our day must still bear that mark. How will we know when we hear a word from the Lord today? We must test it. We must try it. Does it ring with the promise of a good and gracious God who would be all things to His creatures? Does it at the same time thunder against our refusal to take His grace and His blessing? Does it make us feel uneasy because we want to be our own god? Does it ruffle us because we have become pleased with ourselves? Does it tell us that the only solution to ourselves being what we are is to let God be our Salvation through what He reveals to us in Jesus Christ? The touchstone for the prophetic word in Jeremiah's day was the covenant which God had mediated through His servant Moses. The touchstone in our day is the gracious covenant, the new testament which God has mediated through His Son, the Christ. The first mark of the prophetic voice today must be: Does it measure up to this summary of both the old and the new covenant, that we are saved by God's grace alone?

The Prophet Is Willing to Be Sacrificed

The second mark of the prophet is his willingness to die for his cause. This is not a phony kind of martyrdom. It is not a death wish. Jeremiah does not want to die. He wants to live. But if he cannot live to speak the Word he brings, he is willing to be sacrificed for the sake of that Word. He says: "Now therefore amend your ways and your doings, and obey the voice of the Lord your God, and the Lord will repent of the evil which He has pronounced against you. But as for me, behold, I am in your hands. Do with me as seems good and right to you." The true prophet does not go out of his way to build crosses for himself, to be stoned, or to be cut down by the enemy. But he is ready to be offered if the Word itself marks him for the sacrifice.

One cannot divorce this readiness from the Word. There have been many foolish heroes in the world. There has been much insane martyrdom. Many have perished for wrong causes. But Jeremiah does not believe it is necessary for him to die to make his cause good. His cause is right and proper. If men believe the Word of the Lord, they will be spared, and he will be spared. If they do not believe, and they decide to kill him, he hopes that his dying words will echo in their hearts at the time of their destruction.

We have known the likes of this kind of martyrdom in our times — men like Hanns Lilje, who suffered imprisonment, and Dietrich Bonhoeffer, who was hanged by the Nazis. But we need to know it also now in the Word which we hear. The Word which we hear today must also ring with the earnestness of the prophet. We must know that the Word which is preached is matched with the willingness to stand, to live, and to die for it.

When Luther was pressed by his enemies because of his teachings, he wrote:

I do not claim to be a prophet, but I do say that the more they scorn me and the higher they regard themselves, the more reason they have to fear that I may be a prophet. God is marvelous in his works and judgments. He pays attention neither to numbers, greatness, cunning, or power. As Psalm 138 [:6] says: "The haughty he knows from afar." And even if I am not a prophet, as far as I am concerned I am sure that the Word of God is with me and not with them, for I have the Scriptures on my side and they have only their own doctrine. This gives me courage, so that the more they despise and persecute me, the less I fear them." (*Luther's Works*, Vol. 32, p. 9)

This is the kind of courage we must mark in the prophetic voices of today. When this confidence comes from the goodness and grace of God as He has revealed Himself, we may know that God is continuing His prophetic office through the voices of men.

The Prophet Relies on God's Faithfulness

A third mark of the prophet is the prophet's trust that God's Word will ultimately triumph. Because of the nature of his people's unfaith Jeremiah was disposed to speak a harsh word to his people to bring them to repentance. He risked death in doing so. But he said: "Know for certain that if you put me to death, you will bring innocent blood upon yourselves and upon this city and its inhabitants, for in truth the Lord sent me to you to speak all these words in your ears."

The people did not put Jeremiah to death that day, and his life was spared. But, tragically, repentance was not forthcoming. Jeremiah remained in jeopardy during the time of his service until Jerusalem was destroyed. At that time he was carried to Egypt by his fellows, who sought to save him. But even they turned on him because of his teachings and sawed him in pieces. Yet Jeremiah's word had been vindicated. It was a word from the Lord. Jerusalem was destroyed because of this people's unrepentance. And God brought back this people from their captivity. God remained faithful to His covenant as Jeremiah said He would. Then Jeremiah's word became precious in the sight of Israel, and they preserved it in a book. Then they knew that he had been a great prophet.

You can see how all these marks of the prophet are readily discerned in our blessed Lord Himself. His message to Jerusalem was the same as that of Jeremiah. He calls for faith in a God who is gracious, that is, a God who saves us by His own work and not our work. In the holy Gospel for today He rejects the praise of women who beatify the role of His mother. He calls them to faith in the covenant: "Blessed rather are those who hear the Word of God and keep it" (Luke 11:28). So He preached everywhere. But His people rejected His prophetic word, for which He, like Jeremiah, was ready to be offered. He knew He would have to die because of their stubbornness of heart, but He was confident that God's will would prevail. And when He was crucified, His Word was vindicated. God brought forth Jesus from the tomb. And when God raised Jesus from the dead, He demonstrated most clearly that His Word does triumph. This risen Christ is God's Word to us that our life is to be found in Him. Without Him we die eternally. In Him we die that God might raise us unto eternity.

This is the note that must be sounded in the prophetic voice today if we are to know it is of God. The prophetic voice must speak in the face of death with the confidence that God will not leave us in death. Jeremiah knew that God would have to destroy His people to raise them up. Jesus knew that though men in their sin would put Him to death, God would raise Him up from the dead. So the prophetic voice of today must remind us that by His grace in Jesus Christ God is able to raise up unto Himself a holy people out of the dust and ashes of our wasted lives.

Bread That Satisfies

≈§ Ho, everyone who thirsts, come to the waters; and he who has no money, come, buy and eat! Come, buy wine and milk without money and without price. Why do you spend your money for that which is not bread, and your labor for that which does not satisfy? Hearken diligently to Me, and eat what is good, and delight yourselves in fatness. Incline your ear, and come to Me; hear, that your soul may live; and I will make with you an everlasting covenant, My steadfast, sure love for David. Behold, I made him a witness to the peoples, a leader and commander for the peoples. Behold, you shall call nations that you know not, and nations that knew you not shall run to you, because of the Lord your God and of the Holy One of Israel; for He has glorified you. ℰ✤

Isaiah 55:1-5 (RSV)

✺ *Bread That Satisfies* ✺

REGULARLY we are informed that other nations are suffering from food shortages. America suffers from an over-abundance of food. Some would hope that like Joseph of old we would be able to play the role of food distributor to the world. But apparently the means to achieving this role are complicated and difficult. Yet it would be proper and fitting for us all to pray that somehow food could become the symbol of goodwill between nations and the means of solution to precarious international tensions.

If exploration of outer space is considered a means of achieving unity, why should not the exploration of the food problem? Man the world over hungers for food. It is of greatest significance to him. In the Scriptures food plays a significant role as a means of prominent importance. We are reminded of this today in the holy Gospel, the story of Christ Feeding the Multitude, and in the Old Testament lesson, which is an offer of food without a price.

The Bread That Cannot Satisfy

Bread in and of itself cannot satisfy. It is a means of sustenance. But it sustains only the body. It may give physical strength. It may give pleasure to the taste. It may give satisfaction to smell. But it cannot satisfy beyond that. Its limitations are set by man's death. No health food has been raised that carries in it the germ of eternal life. Our Lord pointed this out to the multitude who came to make Him a bread king after the miraculous feeding. They wanted Him to be like Moses, who fed their fathers in the wilderness. He said that it was His Father who fed them. Besides, their fathers were now dead, even though they had eaten manna, that angel food. The full intention of Christ was to point the people beyond the bread, as God had intended to do with His people in the wilderness.

If men fail to understand that bread cannot satisfy in and of itself, they may become slaves of the breadbasket. They will find themselves laboring for something that cannot satisfy in the hope that it will. Bread will be the god whom they serve. One need only go to a modern restaurant to discover the cult of this people at worship. The setting is that of a temple. The appointments and accoutrements are of the finest metals, woods, and fabrics to be found. The chef is the priest, set apart in his holy of holies of gleaming stainless steel. The waitresses are the priestesses waiting upon the needs of their people. And the specified offering is taken on a silver tray. But none seems to mind paying the price, for as they say around the cult, "You have to pay for the atmosphere." Some people live for this life of food service. They are people who hope that the rites with food will satisfy. They live and swear by Duncan Hines. They travel through life making every fine food counter a shrine. But like the children of the wilderness, they, too, will die.

Thus food not only fails to satisfy in and of itself but is a temptation. A great deal of significance must be attached to the fact that the temptation stories have to do with food. Adam is not to lust after a food forbidden to him. Every food which he does eat is more than a food. It is a blessing.

It is accompanied by God's goodwill and pleasure. However, once he tasted of the forbidden fruit, he tasted of a food without God's promise. He ate himself into death. He tasted of death. From that moment on he was to eat his bread by the sweat of his face, and never again could he find a bread that in itself would satisfy. Thus it was that our Lord refused the temptation to think that bread baked out of stones could satisfy His yearning to remain His Father's only Son.

In these temptations we must see how we ourselves are tempted by bread. Bread can become the means of our sorest and worst temptations. It can become the means of our destruction and ruination. We are told that we are eating ourselves to death in America. I am not an authority on overweight, and I am sure there are all kinds of glandular and other reasons for overweight. But is it not true that we are very much guilty in our day of abundance of making food a great temptation? And would it not be the real irony of history that it should be said of us that the most prosperous food-producing nation the world has ever known ate its way to the grave? Be that as it may, the word of the prophet is fitting for us: "Why do you spend your money for that which is not bread, and your labor for that which does not satisfy?" He reminds us as he reminded the exiles of his day: If we labor for bread alone, we shall never be satisfied.

The Bread That Satisfies

To keep his people from longing for the wrong thing, the prophet offers to the exiles of Israel their only true hope, the true bread. The writer here offers consolation. They are the forgiven Israel, a people about to be restored to their former station. The exiles are to return to their home. They will participate in the deliverance reminiscent of when God delivered their fathers from bondage in Egypt. A king will restore the former glory which David brought to Israel. She will be a nation favored above all others. She will be restored because of the promises of God.

In this lesson the writer identifies the promises of God's grace as free water, as wine and milk without price. In the Orient water was precious and sold for a price. We have the picture of a carrier bringing water, milk, and wine, and crying, "Ho, everyone who thirsts, come to the waters, and he who has no money, come, buy and eat! Come, buy wine and milk without money and without price." This offer of God's promises is free. It is grace. There is no price to be paid. You could not buy this plentiful food if you wanted to. These promises are identified with an everlasting covenant which God would make with His people. The Holy One of Israel, the Redeemer God, has vowed by His love for His people to glorify them. In this covenant is found life. This covenant is the food that satisfies the soul. The Old Testament treats the soul as if it were the source of the appetite. In God's grace, in the salvation He provides, the appetite of the soul is satisfied.

Similarly our Lord speaks of Himself as the Bread of Life. We are to eat of Him if we are to be satisfied. He is what we yearn for. We are hungry for life. By faith we are to take Him who is the Fulfillment of God's promises to us. In the Christ God establishes the covenant to give us life. He who eats His flesh and drinks His blood has eternal life, and Jesus will raise him up at the Last Day (John 6:54). This means that when we believe that the flesh and blood of our Lord Jesus Christ is the flesh and blood which was given into death that it might destroy death and bring life to light by the resurrection from the dead, then we already possess eternal life. When we have this, we can be satisfied. Then we have that which the world searches for and is denied unless it looks to the Christ. But we have this precious gift now. We have to look and search no farther, we need not try to earn a different kind of bread than this to satisfy our deepest yearnings. Christ is the Bread of Life that is ours. He is ours without money and without price. He is the Holy One of Israel through whom we are glorified.

Elsewhere in Scripture food is spoken of in a special sacramental way. At the giving of the covenant at Sinai eating and drinking appear to be the seal and the pledge of the covenant (Ex. 24:11). Our Lord Himself instituted His Holy Supper as a seal and pledge of His new testament. He also promises His followers that they shall eat and drink at His table in His kingdom (Luke 22:30). In some of the accounts of the resurrection appearances, Jesus sits down to eat with His disciples, and He "was known to them in the breaking of bread" (Luke 24:35). It is also apparent that immediately after the ascension of our Lord the common meal of the early church was associated with Christ's promised appearance.

These sacramental meals are definitely associated with the promises of God in Christ. This is the eating and drinking which God employs to accommodate Himself to our spiritual appetites. In the Sacrament of the Lord's Supper the cry of the prophet in our lesson is heard again. Here we are able to taste of God's mercy. We are called away from the bread that does not satisfy and from the bread which is not bread. Here the Living Bread of heaven becomes ours in and under the bread. Here the blood which was shed as the pledge of our salvation becomes ours in and under the wine. Before this meal of God we must ask ourselves where our appetites are really fixed. Do we go on believing that somewhere out in the world we will find a bread such as this? Do we believe that we have to pay a price, that we have to earn our salvation through our own merits? Or shall we come to this banquet to feast on God's mercies, which are to be had without a price?

The Scriptures speak of food in yet another way. In the Our Father our Lord Himself has taught us to pray, "Give us this day our daily bread." When you and I pray this petition, we are not to ask God to fill the breadbasket. Luther has rightly pointed out that God does this whether we ask Him or not. What is more, He does this even for the wicked. What we are praying is that God would lead us to understand it and to receive the daily bread with thanksgiving. This means we are to eat our daily bread in the fellowship of our Lord Himself. By this prayer our Lord Jesus takes us by the hand and leads us into the very presence of the heavenly Father. By this prayer we eat at God's table. By this prayer our daily bread — the meat and potatoes too — becomes a gift of God's mercy and His grace. By faith we see that our daily bread, too, becomes a bread that satisfies.

Our Father Abraham

⋖§ *Now the Lord said to Abraham, "Go from your country and your kindred and your father's house to the land that I will show you. And I will make of you a great nation, and I will bless you and make your name great so that you will be a blessing. I will bless those who bless you, and him who curses you I will curse; and by you all the families of the earth will bless themselves."* ৯

Genesis 12:1-3 (RSV)

❧ *Our Father Abraham* ❧

THE holy Gospel for today is a dramatic presentation of a dialog between Jesus and the people in attendance at a Feast of the Tabernacles. The dialog centers on the question of lineage.

> The people claim they are the freeborn sons of Abraham.
>
> Jesus says they are not.
>
> The people claim they are the children of God.
>
> Jesus calls them children of the devil.
>
> The people say Jesus has a demon.
>
> Jesus tells them they do not know God and they are liars; Abraham had rejoiced to see His day and was glad.
>
> The people ask Jesus how He could have seen Abraham, because Jesus was not yet 50 years old.
>
> Jesus answers, "Before Abraham was, I am."
>
> The people pick up stones to kill Jesus because He appears to be a blasphemer. Jesus had dared to call Himself "I Am," the old covenant name for God.

Who was right, Jesus or the people? You will say Jesus, because you claim to be Christian. But that is not enough. This could be as illusionary as the claim of the people whom

Christ comfronted. The drama could very well be a picture of you and the Christ. If you give your answer simply on the basis that you belong to a Christian congregation, you miss the point. What each of us must do is examine carefully the story of Abraham to see what these words of Jesus mean, and then see if we can in all integrity call Abraham our father.

Abraham Is a Child of Faith

What the Lord Christ was saying is that there are two ways in which one could be a child of Abraham. One could be his descendant in the flesh, as these people were. Or one could be his child in the spirit, as these people were not. Jesus faulted them for not being the latter. They had relied on their lineage of the flesh to be counted as the children of God. The Lord Jesus was calling them to an understanding of Abraham as their father in the spirit. Abraham was called to a fatherhood in the spirit. He had received a calling from God to go out from his country, the Ur of the Chaldeans. He was to leave his father's house to go to a land of God's choosing.

We do not know how this call came to Abraham and what form it may have taken. Luther thinks that Shem was a priest at Salem and that he urged Abraham to leave his land. It could be that God had revealed Himself to Abraham through some other person or some other means. Perhaps he was forced to leave because of some dire necessity. Perhaps the call came in some other more dramatic manner. However the call came, it was a call from God. The call was not easy to answer. It meant coming out from his home and everything that had been dear to him. He had to leave his father's house. This meant giving up everything that had gone into making him what he was.

He was to cut himself off from the roots from which he had grown. He was to isolate himself from everything that had been his company. He was to tear himself away from the things to which he had become attached. He is called out from an old life to a new life.

But why is he called out? He is called out from idolatrous practices in the Ur of the Chaldeans. Ur was a land of culture and sophistication. It was a land not devoid of rule and orderliness. But it was a land that did not make God the center of its life. It had reduced its gods to the stature of things made by hands. It had converted its way of life into its peculiar kind of godliness. It tried to make the good things it knew, liked, and counted dear into something godly. It made its gods out of the substance of the creation. So many do this day. They fix themselves to the creation. They would draw out of it the gods they worship. Our generation makes religion of humanism, scientism, or nationalism, and anything else it chooses. But to make religion of these things, to make idols of them, is to know not God.

Thus it was that God called out Abraham, called out one who, too, may have been an idolater. (Luther interprets Joshua 24:2 to include Abraham.) By His Word God seized on Abraham to take him out of a world that was His creation but in which men no longer knew Him as Creator. By His call through the Word He would recreate Abraham. God would take him to a new land and make of him a new people. This is how God creates His holy church. He calls us out from the life in which we are in bondage to the things of this world. He calls us out from the slavery of a life that is bound to the creation but not to the Creator. Thus the church is quite properly called in the Greek the *ekklesia,* those who are called out. We are called out from the world that knows not the grace and mercy of God to trust in the good and gracious God who is the God of Abraham.

By this call God intends to make of Abraham a great blessing to others. "I will make of you a great nation, and I will bless you and make your name great so that you will be a blessing." God has a plan which He intends to set in motion through Abraham. Abraham is to become the agent of God's mercies. He is to become an ambassador of God's grace. He is to become the patriarch of God's family. This hardly seems likely. Abraham is already 75 years old. Sarah is 65, and they are childless. Everything appears to work against any notion that Abraham and Sarah are to have offspring, let alone a great nation. Any sensible, reasonable person would say that the idea was a wild dream. How it was that Abraham believed that his calling to a new land would result in the establishment of a new nation in his name is remarkable. Yet believe he did. He packed his belongings and left in search of the new land. Hoping against hope he began the wanderings of a nomad, a sheik of faith on a pilgrimage of promise.

So God always sets His great men of faith in motion. The heroes of God do not move on a stage of smashing successes and bright prospects. They work with the odds all against them. They can stand alone against the world. They can come out from under all the security they know to risk everything for the sake of what God calls them to be. Thus the church appears to the world to be anemic, weak, and helpless. And often our God permits us to look this hopeless. Many times we are called to stand alone in the world. Our situation appears futile. We feel isolated and desolate. Like Abraham we appear to stand against the world. Yet

167

in our predicament God works to make us a blessing. As God did begin the history of a great nation with this man of faith, so God is able to employ our faith as a blessing to others. By our faith we are to serve. God has called us to be a blessing. Thus as we see ourselves as those called by God out from the world to be a special blessing to the world, we stand in the lineage of our father Abraham.

Abraham's Children Are of the Faith

However, the people to whom Jesus addressed Himself at the Feast of the Tabernacles would have agreed with as much as has been said about the relationship to Abraham. In fact, this is the point they would have pushed. They identified Abraham as the father of a special people, a called-out people. They were this people, and they wanted the whole world to know it. They were exclusively this people. They had developed an intense sense of nationalism because of Abraham. Particularly since the return of the people from Babylon had they deepened this feeling. They had shut themselves off from everyone else. Even those who were related to them, such as the Samaritans, were despised by them. Consequently, when the people accuse Jesus of being a Samaritan, they identify Him as an enemy, an outsider. They could point with pride to the promise made to the father Abraham. The promise, they claimed, referred to them: "I will bless those who bless you, and him who curses you I will curse; and by you all the families of the earth will bless themselves." They were the nation that was to be a blessing to those who would believe just as they did. They were the nation that would be a judgment upon all those who did not believe as they did.

But what did they believe? What was the promise which

had been given to Abraham? In what sense could he be
a blessing? Certainly it could not be in what Abraham was
doing or would do. Abraham's works were not the source
of blessing. And this is the point of contention that Jesus
made with the people at the feast. They had made their
possession of the Law their pride. They counted themselves children of Abraham, and their inheritance was the
Law. But the Lord Jesus and later the apostle Paul pointed
out that it was not by the Law that Abraham had been
called to be their father. It was by promise that he was
called. And it was by faith that he went. The "Law came
after," says Paul. "Thus Abraham believed God, and it was
reckoned to him as righteousness" (Gal. 3:6). It had to be
obvious that the promise could not be accomplished in
Abraham's day. He would not see the great nation. Therefore he could not be the one who would be making the
blessing of others. That was strictly God's doing. If there
was to be any blessing of the world through his seed, his
offspring, it would be because of this very promise of God.
It would be God who created the blessing. Abraham was
simply believing the promise which God in His grace made
to him. Abraham himself would be blessed through the
promise which he believed.

This is what our Lord meant when He said: "Your father
Abraham rejoiced that he was to see My day; he saw it and
was glad" (John 8:56). Christ is the Fulfillment of the
promise, but He is also the Promise. The promise has the
same effect. God makes Abraham His son through the
promise. And when Abraham had his son Isaac, he recognized him as a sign of God's faithfulness. By believing the
promise, Abraham, Luther says, receives that "great and

inexpressible gift" that he should be "physically the father of the Son of God" (*Luther's Works*, Vol. 2, p. 248). By believing this promise Abraham enters into a history that culminates in the birth, death, and resurrection of our Lord. And these are the actions of God in the history of the progeny of Abraham that are to be for the blessing or cursing of the nations. Because Abraham believed that God would provide the blessing, he was blessed. Because he believed that God was the Center of life, he had found life. Because he believed that he needed to be rescued from the life of idolatry, God had become his Savior. He had seen the "day" of our Lord "and was glad."

Now you see this is how we become the children of our father Abraham. We become his children by faith also. We are drawn to our God by the same promise, by the same grace, the same call, and the same Lord Christ. As Paul writes, "It is men of faith who are the sons of Abraham. And the Scripture, foreseeing that God would justify the Gentiles by faith, preached the Gospel beforehand to Abraham, saying, 'In thee shall all the nations be blessed.' So then those who are men of faith are blessed with Abraham, who had faith" (Gal. 3:7-9). We then may rightfully claim Abraham as our father. God's promise to Abraham is for all men. His children are the holy church. The children who have come from his loins are not his children in the spiritual sense unless they, too, trust this good and gracious God.

But do you also see what burden this claim lays on us? We need also to live by faith. We can rest on no false claim to being the children of Abraham. We are not his because we belong to this congregation or because we were confirmed in the church or because our grandmother was

a Christian or because we have the Law or because we have
the Scriptures or because we possess orthodox confessions.
To be the children of Abraham, we must answer the call
of God's voice and live by faith. We must live by faith in
Him who was before Abraham.

The Messianic King Comes

꿟 Rejoice greatly, O daughter of Zion! Shout aloud, O daughter of Jerusalem! Lo, your King comes to you; triumphant and victorious is He, humble and riding on an ass, on a colt, the foal of an ass. I will cut off the chariot from Ephraim and the war horse from Jerusalem; and the battle bow shall be cut off, and He shall command peace to the nations; His dominion shall be from sea to sea and from the River to the ends of the earth. As for you also, because of the blood of My covenant with you, I will set your captives free from the waterless pit. Return to your stronghold, O prisoners of hope; today I declare that I will restore to you double. ੨ઌ

Zechariah 9:9-12 (RSV)

❧ *The Messianic King Comes* ❧

THIS was the zero hour. Jesus made entry into the city of Jerusalem to do battle with the final enemy — death. The manner of His entry was significant. It was deliberately planned and open. The manner of entry was a radical departure from the previous painstaking attempts to hide His Messiahship from political abuses. On occasion He had strictly forbidden people to tell anyone He was the Christ (Matt. 16:20). When He raised Jairus' daughter, He charged the people to tell nobody (Mark 5:43). At His transfiguration He warned His disciples to tell no one (Mark 9:8). After the feeding of the multitude He withdrew from the people when they wanted to make Him king (John 6:15). The Gospel according to John carries the repeated refrain that His hour was not yet come (John 7:6). In addition to this, our Lord employed the Messianic name "Son of Man" when He referred to Himself. This Messianic title was the least controversial and least political in His day. The title veiled His mission and yet identified it.

The entry into Jerusalem, however, was a bold stroke. Jesus comes to the city with all the marks and signs of the Messianic King mentioned in the prophetic book Zechariah. This prophetic word is of a late date. It comes from that period after the restoration following the Babylonian Cap-

tivity when the Messianic hopes of the people were inten-
sified. The Messianic expectations took definite shape and
form, and the prophecy of the Messianic King gives us
a notion of the high expectation that filled the later period.
There are some who have surmised that the historical incident that suggested the vision of the Messianic King was the
procession of Alexander the Great. That may but need
not be. The hope here presented represents by itself that
strong anticipation of the appearance of the Messianic King.
As such it represents what the people of the Covenant could
expect of their Messianic King.

He Comes as Victorious

The Messianic King who comes in the name of the Lord
fulfills all the expectations of God's people. "Lo, your King
comes to you; triumphant and victorious is He." The Gospel
according to Matthew identifies this King as the Lord Jesus
Christ. The writer, however, does not quote the words
"triumphant and victorious is He." This is understandable
since these words would not have fit his story at this point.
The evangelist is intent on describing the humility of the
Lord Jesus. Yet it is true that Jesus enters the city triumphant and victorious. Already He had gained significant
battles on the field. He had scored significant victories over
the tempters. He had foiled those who had tried to destroy
His effectiveness as a rabbi. He had squelched those who
tried to entangle Him in His speech. He had avoided those
who desired Him to make selfish use of His abilities. He had
escaped those who offered Him high honor if He would
serve their purposes. He had overwhelmed these enemies.
He had thrust aside every temptation that threatens to
darken the soul. He could say to His disciples that the
ruler of this world, Satan, was judged. (John 16:11)

These were signal victories. These were holy triumphs. We need this kind of deliverance. We need our Messianic King to break the stranglehold which the world has on us. We need to be set free from the bondage to conceit and deceit. We need to be led out of the maze of temptations that lead us from one lie to another. We need to be liberated from the slavery to our own weaknesses. We need to be rescued from the notion that we must settle for being what we are. We need to be saved from the deadening effects of our guilt, from the killing aspects of doubt and the numbed sensations of fear. We desperately need a victory. We need a winner. We need the Messianic King to come to us as One who is victorious and triumphant for our sakes. We need to know that He has laid low the power of those forces which seek to destroy our identity as the creatures of God.

As the Christ enters Jerusalem, He comes with the assurance of these victories and these triumphs. He comes in confidence and trust that He has accomplished much in life for us. The honesty, integrity, and holiness which He had preserved under the stress of temptation is the holiness which He may share with His followers. He had come to demonstrate that His Father, the Creator, was the Ruler of man. He had come to expose the rulers of evil as empty in the face of His goodness. He had come to put out the powers of darkness with the Light of His Father's grace. As the Messianic King comes to us with these victories, we are to receive Him in faith. We may receive Him in the joy that He reestablishes for us the truth that we need not yield ourselves to the temptations of the world. Instead we may give ourselves to Him who has destroyed the enemy for us.

He Comes Through the Unexpected

As we study the vision of the coming of the Messianic King, we see that He accomplished our expectations through the unexpected. Triumphant and victorious as He is, He comes "humble and riding on an ass, on a colt, the foal of an ass." He does not come on a war horse. He does not come on a prancing steed. He does not come in the pomp of a Saul, the power of a David, or the glamor of a Solomon. This Messianic King chooses to ride a quiet, placid, homely ass. God chooses to ride an ass, which is to be a symbol of the manner in which He gains His victory and establishes His kingdom. One would expect this King to win great victories by His vast power. One would expect Him to gain smashing victories by exercising His force. One would expect Him to destroy all of the opposition with one mighty blow. And as He comes to His city, to His people, in triumph, one would expect Him to appear in a glorious light, a show of power, a display of might. Instead the ass is the symbol of His lowliness, His humility. He comes as King, to be sure, but a King who will not rule by brute force but who desires to rule His people by love. He comes not to put to death all who are His enemies. But He comes to save His enemies by suffering death at their hands.

He comes to "cut off the chariot from Ephraim and the war horse from Jerusalem; and the battle bow shall be cut off." He comes to reverse the conditions that had prevailed. Ephraim had been the Northern Kingdom, which had been destroyed in the eighth century before Christ. Jerusalem had been destroyed in the sixth century before Christ. The destruction of these kingdoms had been God's judgment upon the kingdoms for their failure to live under the covenant. The Messianic King came to reverse these

177

judgments for their sin. He came to reconcile these people to their God. He came to restore the covenant. He came to assure them that their God desired to make peace with them and to keep the powers of destruction from their gates. He comes in peace to restore peace. He comes to make this people at one with their God. He comes to "command peace to the nations." He would establish peace again by His command, by His Word.

So Jesus, the Messianic King, did come to Jerusalem. He came to these people to bring them peace. He came to win the peace for them by love and not by power. They did not recognize Him or believe Him. The crowd thought He would be a political leader. The religious leaders despised His Messiahship of grace. They wanted a messiah by the Law. And so they crucified Him. They knew Him not, for their expectations were different. He did the unexpected. But had they remembered the word and the expectations of the prophet, they would have known and believed Him that Palm Sunday afternoon.

He Fulfills the Covenant

When the Messianic King comes, He comes because of the covenant which He has made with His people. "As for you also, because of the blood of My covenant with you, I will set your captives free from the waterless pit. Return to your stronghold, O prisoners of hope; today I declare that I will restore to you double." God's decision to come as the Messianic King is neither a new nor a novel idea. His coming is wholly consistent with the manner in which He has always dealt with His people. He abides by the covenant which He has made with them. That covenant had been sealed with blood as Moses sprinkled the blood of the peace offering upon the people (Ex. 24:7, 8). The sacrifice was the assurance that God by His grace provided the sacrifice for the sins of the people. The blood, which to the Hebrew is the seat of life, was the assurance that God had granted to His people new life in the covenant. Thus when the Messianic King comes, He comes as the faithful Keeper of His covenant. He comes that He might spring His people loose from their bondage to a life alien to the covenant. He comes to set the captives free. He comes to loose the prisoners from the chains of death. He comes to grant them new life.

Thus when our Lord Jesus came because of the blood of the old covenant, the blood which He shed at Calvary became the blood of the new covenant. His sacrifice is the pledge of God's faithfulness to His new testament. By this offering of Himself on the cross He gives unconditional guarantee and assurance to us that He has come to set us free from our bondage under the old life. We need never fear. We need never doubt that God will leave us isolated and cut off from His forgiveness and grace. God's offering of love is ours forever. We have new life because He has come.

Our Lord makes this pledge all the more secure for us in the Sacrament of the Altar. In the sacrament He does not sprinkle us with the blood of Calvary. In the sacrament, however, He does permit us to partake of that blood of the new testament that we might know that in the receiving of this blood we have taken to ourselves life and salvation.

As the Messianic King comes to us today in His Word and sacrament, may we receive Him in true faith and full reverence as we greet Him in the word of the Sanctus: "Blessed is He that cometh in the name of the Lord. Hosanna, Hosanna in the highest!"

⋘ *As they were saying this, Jesus Himself stood among them. But they were startled and frightened and supposed that they saw a spirit. And He said to them, "Why are you troubled, and why do questionings rise in your hearts? See My hands and My feet, that it is I Myself; handle Me and see; for a spirit has not flesh and bones as you see that I have." And while they still disbelieved for joy and wondered, He said to them, "Have you anything here to eat?" They gave Him a piece of broiled fish, and He took it and ate before them.*

Then He said to them, "These are My words which I spoke to you while I was still with you, that everything written about Me in the Law of Moses and the Prophets and the Psalms must be fulfilled." Then He opened their minds to understand the Scriptures and said to them, "Thus it is written, that the Christ should suffer and on the third day rise from the dead and that repentance and forgiveness of sins should be preached in His name to all nations, beginning from Jerusalem." ⋙

Luke 24:36-47 (RSV)

✌§ The Easter Gospel §✧

WE Americans can boast that we have been able to launch satellites into orbits we have fixed for them. The effect of this feat cannot be measured. We have broken the system of time and space that we knew. We have created something that has become a part of spacelessness and timelessness. Yet the Easter Gospel of Luke asserts that this is not the great news of history. The great moment of history occurred when One came out of eternity to break the old system of time and space.

In the Christ the God of eternity has entered our closed system. Our system was closed when man slammed the door on God's eternity by his sin and entered the closed system of time and death. Man can never escape the problem of time and death by his attempt to break into outer space and timelessness. However, we do know that in Christ God came to this creation to make a breakthrough to eternity for all men. It is this news that Easter proclaims to us.

A Call to Faith

The proclamation of the Easter Gospel is filled with signs of the resurrection. In the Johannine Gospel we hear that as Mary Magdalene stood by the tomb, it was by a word from our Lord that she recognized the risen Christ. In the

Lukan Easter Gospel we see how the Lord gives definite signs to His disciples for their faith. The crucified Lord who stands among them is risen. Is He who appears among them simply a specter or vision? Were the disciples so far wrong when they supposed that they had seen a spirit? If the devil himself can camouflage himself as an angel of light, could he not also create a vision of being Christ? Or are the appearances of this Crucified One simply apparitions produced by the longing of tortured hearts of disciples? In the Lukan Gospel the Christ makes sure His disciples do not delude themselves. He gives them signs. He says: "See My hands and My feet, that it is I Myself." He permits a close examination. "A spirit has not flesh and bones as you see that I have." These were the unexpected signs. He showed hands and feet that bore in them the scars of death.

What does this mean? The risen Lord is not like the Lord who walked from the manger to the cross. Suddenly the risen Christ stood in the midst of the disciples even before they could have noticed Him coming. The Gospel narrates that He came to them through closed doors and stepped into their midst to proclaim His greeting. He appears mysteriously. He disappears mysteriously. He is not immediately recognized, and yet He is recognized beyond a shadow of a doubt. The risen Christ comes to them hidden in the resurrected body, yet manifest as never before. He is distant and yet intimate. Thus He who was placed into the grave a natural corpse is raised a spiritual body (1 Cor. 15:44). There is something quite different. The Christ is so different that His appearances seem to defy proper and full description of even those who witnessed the appearances. And yet they witnessed them.

At this point we are apt to launch off into some kind of defense of how it could be that the Lord Jesus could be risen from the dead. Perhaps we could go to the scientists and have them admit that the scientific method is incapable of constructing a complete explanation of nature. If somehow we could get an admission from the scientific world that the resurrection is possible, then perhaps it would not be so difficult to believe in the resurrection. However, this would be to miss the point of the resurrection Gospel. The evangelist says that the disciples "still disbelieved for joy and wondered." Those who reported to be witnesses didn't believe themselves. The scientific method, the proof itself, did not work for them. The point is that we are so used to living in a closed system that we are completely overwhelmed by Him who came to break the barriers to that system. We are so accustomed to death's claim on us that we are disturbed by Him who comes to destroy that claim. We are so adapted to living with our guilt that we are frightened by One so holy that death could not contain Him. It is our sin and our shame that cause us disbelief and wonder at the hearing of the resurrection Gospel. It is only proper then that this Easter Gospel puts the offense of our disbelief where it belongs. The Lord Jesus points to His hands and His feet, which bear the marks of His crucifixion. The scars of the Christ should bring terror to our hearts, for the Easter Gospel would remind us that it was for us that this Christ died. It was our sins against the Father that sent Him to the cross. It was for us that the Father raised Him from the dead. This then is how this Easter Gospel would call us to faith. We are asked to behold His hands and His feet and thereby be reminded that it was because of us that the risen Christ has gone to the grave.

An Offer of Life

This Easter Gospel would also have us notice that the resurrection of Jesus Christ is a phenomenon different from the raising of other people mentioned in the Gospels. The evangelists relate that Jesus raised Jairus' daughter, the young man at Nain, and Lazarus. Jesus, however, did not come from death as did these others. The disciples did not come to raise Him from the dead. The Father raised Him from the dead. The Lord Jesus took up His life again as He had promised. Yet the difference is greater than this. The resurrection of others was only a continuation of earthly life for a time till death claimed them once more and they became corpses for the second time. But Jesus, being raised from the dead, dies no more. Death has no more dominion over Him. In that He died, He died unto sin once. In that He lives, He lives unto God (Rom. 6:9, 10). This was the death of death, the resurrection unto life everlasting. When Jesus arose, He snatched the power of death from death itself.

The crucified Christ, who rose in a manner we cannot describe, rose as the New Man, the Second Adam. The risen Lord is different from us sinners after the Fall, different also from Adam before the Fall. He is the other — the Second Adam. And so it is written, "The first man, Adam, became a living being," and the Second Adam became a life-giving spirit. The first Adam was of the earth; the Second Adam is the Lord from heaven (1 Cor. 15:45). The first man was created by God to live eternally in the obedience of faith. Jesus Christ, however, is the other Man, who is the first to obtain this life by believing and being obedient unto death. All men before Him failed to reach this life because all sinned against God. They remained in the earthly sphere from which God took their bodies, and they were held fast there as sinners. At death they were sealed in their curse. But Jesus did not overcome the sinners in the world to leave them behind. He did not rise only for Himself. He did not clutch His own resurrection firmly in His hands as if it were a prize reserved for Him. No sooner had He escaped death than the Lord returned to those who had deserted and forsaken Him in death. As soon as He had frustrated the world in its enmity, He extended His hands to offer Himself in His resurrection to the world.

This is what this Easter Gospel should mean to us. We have deserted and forsaken our Lord day in and day out. We have deserted Him when the demands were great and when the demands were small. We have failed to walk as obedient children. We have failed to serve Him with faithfulness. We have failed to surrender ourselves to Him totally and completely. We have failed to listen to His Word and trust His meaning. We have failed to live in the confidence that where He takes us can be only to the good. And yet He returns to us as a faithful and forgiving Lord. He returns to us to share His victory with us. He returns to us to give us life. He returns to us to destroy the shadows of death.

A Sign of Hope

The Lukan Gospel records yet another side that should be of great significance to us. The Lord Jesus understands the frailty and feebleness of faith of His disciples. He asks that they bring Him something to eat. They bring Him a broiled fish. He eats so that they might know that the Christ who sits among them is the Christ they had known before. The risen Christ sits down to eat with old friends and to break bread with them. The risen Christ identifies

Himself with the old creation and the old creatures. He is ready and willing to draw men unto Himself, and as He takes the food, His friends might know that He is willing to take them unto Himself.

And so you and I may come to this altar today for the same purpose. We know this Christ and Lord of all. We know the Christ who is risen. He is not contained by space or by time. He has broken through time and our closed system so that He might bring eternity to us. Christ comes today. He is willing to break bread with us as a sign that He breaks bread of the old creation that we might be drawn into the new. We who are of the old system of closed time and death are able to taste of the new. We still stand here in the old creation face to face with time and death. Yet we are able to receive here at this altar the body and blood of our Lord. As we take Him, we are become a part of the new system of life and resurrection. Come then and refresh your hearts with the assurance that as we break bread today we are being brought into the breadth of eternity.

The Fulfillment of the Prophets

The Lukan Easter Gospel also adds: "Then He [Jesus] said to them, 'These are My words which I spoke to you while I was still with you, that everything written about Me in the Law of Moses and the Prophets and the Psalms must be fulfilled.' Then He opened their minds to understand the Scriptures and said to them, 'Thus it is written, that the Christ should suffer and on the third day rise from the dead and that repentance and forgiveness of sins should be preached in His name to all nations, beginning from Jerusalem.'"

Here is how we see that the Easter faith begins to dawn

upon the faithful. The attestation to the resurrection of Jesus Christ is not found in more and more appearances but in that which had already been revealed. They are called to faith in this risen Christ by what God had revealed He would do for His people. Through the mouth of His servant Moses this God is heard to say: "The eternal God is your Dwelling Place, and underneath are the everlasting arms." (Deut. 33:27)

The prophet spoke for this God: "Shall I ransom them from the power of Sheol? Shall I redeem them from Death? O Death, where are your plagues? O Sheol, where is your destruction?" (Hos. 13:14)

The psalmist says of this God: "For Thou dost not give Me up to Sheol or let Thy Godly One see the Pit." (Ps. 16:10)

In the risen Christ the faithful come to understand the meaning of such words. In the Word the faithful come to understand the risen Christ. And what is it that the risen Christ should mean to us? "That repentance and forgiveness of sins should be preached in His name to all nations, beginning from Jerusalem." This is genuine Easter faith. It is to know that in the risen Christ God comes to us to call us to repentance and to accept His forgiveness. This Easter we are called on once again to empty ourselves of the death of our former selves and to take the new life He offers in the Christ.

In *The Seven That Were Hanged and Other Stories* Leonid Andreyev tells the story of the minister of government who is to be assassinated. The assassination plot is discovered, and the guards of the minister tell him that he is to be killed at one o'clock the next afternoon. The information distresses the minister so greatly that he cannot sleep. He says over and over to himself that to die is not so terrible. The terrible thing is for one to know that one is going to die. It would be dreadful for a man to know the hour and day of his death with absolute certainty. The still greater terror for man is that by reason of his sins he knows he has his death coming to him. It is this terror that Christ has removed from our lives by His resurrection. The Easter Gospel is the assurance to us that the breakthrough to eternity has been made. Even if we were to know the hour and day of death with absolute certainty, this we would know more surely, that He who has gone before us into death will also lead us into His eternity.

The Victory of Faith

◄§ *The same night he arose and took his two wives, his two maids, and his eleven children and crossed the ford of the Jabbok. He took them and sent them across the stream, and likewise everything that he had. And Jacob was left alone; and a man wrestled with him until the breaking of the day. When the man saw that He did not prevail against Jacob, He touched the hollow of his thigh; and Jacob's thigh was put out of joint as he wrestled with Him. Then He said, "Let Me go, for the day is breaking." But Jacob said, "I will not let You go unless You bless me." And He said to him, "What is your name?" And he said, "Jacob." Then He said, "Your name shall no more be called Jacob, but Israel, for you have striven with God and with men and have prevailed." Then Jacob asked Him, "Tell me, I pray, Your name." But He said, "Why is it that you ask My name?" And there He blessed him. So Jacob called the name of the place Peniel, saying, "For I have seen God face to face, and yet my life is preserved." §►*

Genesis 32:22-30 (RSV)

⊷ *The Victory of Faith* ⊱

THIS very ancient and wonderful story is the story of the struggle of faith, the struggle of Jacob's faith. Christian preachers throughout the history of the church have preached on this text as a type of a struggle of our Lord and Savior Jesus Christ. They have seen in the struggle of Jacob the struggle of our Lord. And you and I should also see in this struggle the same kind of struggle that we must make as we wrestle with our God in faith. But this is also the story of the victory of faith.

The Anxiety

You will recall the story of Jacob. You remember the son of Isaac had received the blessing of Isaac. But you will recall also that he had received this blessing because he deceived his father. Normally, according to custom, his brother Esau should have received the blessing. Esau was his twin brother and also the firstborn. But for a mess of pottage he had sold his "legal" rights, according to which he should have received the inheritance of that blessing. The Lord Himself had told Rebekah: "The older shall serve the younger." Jacob's mother saw that Jacob was better equipped spiritually for the reception of his grand blessing, and therefore she worked out a device with him to receive the blessing from the hand of his father. After he had

192

received the blessing he had to flee his home for fear of his life. He went to his uncle Laban, where he worked for many years. There again he experienced blessing, but he also had to wrestle with his uncle in order to obtain blessing in that land. Now, many years later, he has a large family. He is a wealthy man. He plans to return to the land of his father. He comes with his large entourage of cattle, servants, and family. He comes to the brook Jabbok. His servants go out to survey the situation, and they see that Esau is in waiting. He is encamped with an army. Jacob, of course, believes that this is a threat to his life and the life of his family. He sends his family across the stream. He remains on the north side of the brook to think and to meditate. He offers himself to God in prayer.

In the course of his meditation and prayer there comes a man to wrestle with him. It soon appears who this mysterious opponent is: the Lord. The writer calls the opponent a man. The prophet Hosea calls him an angel. Jacob himself says that he has wrestled with God. The opponent is one with whom he wrestles because of everything that has now confronted him. In this precise moment of his life everything becomes important. Everything is gathered up. This is one of those decisive moments in life that come when man has to review everything that he believes in, everything that he has worked for, everything that he has hoped for. All is at stake. It is one of those moments when one's guilt and shame weigh on him and at the same time his hopes and his faith become the largest and the greatest. It is one of those moments when one remembers how much he has deceived people and God, and one wonders and remembers how much he has also relied upon men and relied upon his God. The way in which he is to greet this situation, the way in which he is able to meet it will determine how his family is to survive, how he himself is to survive, how the promise which he bears in his heart is to survive. Everything is expendable in this one circumstance, in this one situation.

Often in our lives we come to such moments. We come to that moment when we, too, realize that everything is under judgment. Our hopes, our dreams, our ambitions are all laid on the block. The way in which we have lived is paraded before us. The thoughts and the memories of the past become important to us. We feel weighted down with shame. We feel weighted down with sin and guilt. At the same time our hearts swell with the hope that God will rescue us. We pray that somehow our faith would not have been in vain. We pray that somehow our faith would become larger than our doubts and our fears and our anxieties. In such a moment we are at the mercy of our God. At such a moment we either live or we die. Our hopes, our dreams, our ambitions will die if God will not carry us through. On the other hand, we are very much alive if God would be responsive to our prayers and to our faith.

Our Lord Jesus Christ Himself knew such a moment. He knew that moment of great struggle in the garden of Gethsemane. There in the garden He had to pray that God might remove this cup of suffering from Him. At the same time He realized that everything was riding on the way in which He met this hour. The hopes of His ministry, the hope of His ministration, the message which He had preached, and the message which He carried in His heart was riding on this hour and the way in which He was going to meet it. He prayed to God that He would strengthen Him for it. The future of the world, the future of the people of God depended on it. He prayed to the Father that He would hold Him, that He would sustain Him. The Christ knows the depths of great spiritual struggle. He entered into the arena of our struggles with us. His Gethsemane was like Jacob's Jabbok. Our Gethsemanes are paved with the sweat of His struggle.

The Struggle

Jacob wrestled with a man, he would not let Him go. He held on to Him, he would not let Him go out of his sight until He had given him a blessing. As he struggled with Him, he realized that this struggle had now become a great spiritual struggle. It had become a great spiritual experience for him. His wrestling became a bout with God. He knew that he could not let this Man go until he had received a blessing. Jacob was the man who had received a blessing from God by the promise which he had received from his father. Jacob was a man who had experienced the blessings of that relationship of the promise with God during the years that he had been with his uncle. Jacob was the man who had prayed on the basis of that promise just the day before. But now he needed to know that there was a blessing in that promise for him. He could not let go of the Man. He held on to Him tenaciously. He struggled hard to wrest from Him the assurance that on the morrow the promise would bring its blessing. On the morrow he hoped the good and gracious God would give him evidence of His grace.

So we are to hold on to our God. As we wrestle with Him in prayer, we are to hold on to Him and get from Him the promise that He will not let go of us. We are called in our hour of prayer to ask this God to remember every good promise which He has ever made to us. We are to hang on to Him and hold Him to every good and gracious act He has ever performed in the world. We are to ask Him to perform His good and His gracious act in us. We are to hold this God to this — that He would be known as a good and gracious God by the way in which He deals with us. This is the call of our prayer and of our faith.

Our Lord Jesus Christ wrestled thus with the Father. He came up from His prayer in Gethsemane to cross over the brook to go to death. He would not let God go. He struggled and He held. He struggled with God and He held on to the promise which He had made to Him, His Son. He would not let go of God even in death. He held on to this God firmly. He held on to this God in that bitter moment when He had to wrestle with death itself. In wrestling with death He was wrestling with God. In His last breath He said, "Father, into Thy hands I commend My spirit." He held on to God, and in so doing He was saying, "I will not go unless Thou bless Me." In that struggle to the last He was asking a blessing for all of us. He was holding God to the promise to bless us in our death.

The Blessing

God blessed Jacob. The Man who wrestled with Jacob touched him on the hollow of his thigh and impaired Jacob so that he had to limp from that day on. But in that impairment, in the wound that came to Jacob, he was now blessed. He was scarred for life. He was maimed for life. Yet he was blessed for life. He had prevailed. He had received a blessing from this Man. He had received a blessing from his God. He would say, "I have seen God face to face, and yet my life is preserved." He had managed to stand before God and receive a blessing of God. He could

know that God is a gracious God. So he became a blessing
to his family and to a whole nation of people. He carried
in his life the blessing of the good and gracious God who
makes Himself known in the covenant of His grace. Thus
Jacob received a new name that early morning. He had
been named Jacob, "heel snatcher." Now he was to be
known as Israel, "one who had striven with God."

Our Lord Jesus Christ did not escape injury. He was
bruised and scarred. He was touched by death. He received a blessing from the Father. God "raised Him from
the dead and made Him sit at His right hand in the heavenly
places, far above all rule and authority and power and dominion and above every name that is named, not only in
this age but also in that which is to come; and He has put
all things under His feet and has made Him the Head over
all things for the church, which is His body, the fullness of
Him who fills all in all" (Eph. 1:20-23). The risen Christ is
the fulfillment of our prayers and our hopes. In Him our
faith in God is not in vain. Through the Christ we may
hold to God in confident hope, sure of His mercy and
His grace.

However, we cannot expect to come from the wrestling
unscarred or unmaimed. Often only through the intense
struggle of faith in great tribulation or sorrow, in deep
depression or inner pain, do we wrestle with this good and
gracious God. But when we hold to Him and trust, we
may bear scars and wounds, we may be maimed, or we
may have suffered less, but we have gained the victory.
In the struggle that makes us cling to Him in faith we have
gained a blessing. We have faced God in all our weakness,
but our life is preserved by His grace. And we have this
assurance in Christ that when we are brought low by death

itself, He will permit us to rise again to see the rosy dawn of His eternity. When we wrestle thus in faith with our God, He gives to us a new nature, and we are the new "Israel," for we have striven with our God and have prevailed.

Jehovah Is the Good Shepherd

◄§ For thus says the Lord God: Behold, I, I Myself will search for My sheep and will seek them out. As a shepherd seeks out his flock when some of his sheep have been scattered abroad, so will I seek out My sheep; and I will rescue them from all places where they have been scattered on a day of clouds and thick darkness. And I will bring them out from the peoples and gather them from the countries and will bring them into their own land; and I will feed them on the mountains of Israel, by the fountains, and in all the inhabited places of the country. I will feed them with good pasture, and upon the mountain heights of Israel shall be their pasture; there they shall lie down in good grazing land, and on fat pasture they shall feed on the mountains of Israel. I Myself will be the Shepherd of My sheep, and I will make them lie down, says the Lord God. I will seek the lost, and I will bring back the strayed, and I will bind up the crippled, and I will strengthen the weak, and the fat and the strong I will watch over; I will feed them in justice. §►

Ezekiel 34:11-16 (RSV)

⋗ Jehovah Is the Good Shepherd ⋖

IN this period of the church's history we are apt to blame the world for all the problems of the church. In the world situation nationalism is a threat to the missionary enterprise of the church. Certain countries are apt to persecute the church. Scientism and materialism are threats to the church. We look outside of us and we see that there are threats of various kinds and sorts which are dire threats to the life of the church. Any failure that the church has we are apt to blame on forces that appear to be on the outside.

It is not so with the prophet. The prophet does not believe that the disturbances are all from without. He believes firmly that the disturbances for the most part come from within. If there is any worldliness, it is also to be found within the life of the church. If there has been any failure, it has been also on the part of the church and the ministers of the church. The failures have come because the people have not realized who they are, nor have the shepherds realized who they are. Consequently the prophet speaks a word that falls hard on the ears of the shepherds. This word is a judgment of the shepherds. But it is also a word which reminds us that God Himself is the true Shepherd. We need to hear this Word. We need to think hard about it and see how it should affect the life of the church today.

The Failure of the Shepherds

The prophets came to remind the people that God is the God of the covenant, the God who is faithful to His people. Here the prophet had to speak out against the ministers of his day in Israel, the shepherds. This word of the prophet says to the shepherds: "You have not performed in faithfulness the task which God has given you to do. You have failed utterly. God has entrusted to you a gracious and a good Word — His covenant, the means by which to save and nurture and help His people. The flock is God's people. There should be no difficulty in keeping this flock as God's people if you would use the Word which God has given. If you would use this gracious and forgiving and sustaining Word, then the flock should stay and remain as God's people." But the flock did not remain. It was scattered. The shepherds had failed.

What had the shepherds failed in? The prophet says to them: "The weak you have not strengthened, the sick you have not healed, the crippled you have not bound up, the strayed you have not brought back, the lost you have not sought, and with force and harshness you have ruled them" (34:4). So the ministers of God's covenant had failed to go out after the people in their miseries and in their woes. The ministers had failed to minister to the people when they needed it the most. They needed a word of grace when they were guilty. They needed a word of comfort when they were frightened. They needed a word of protection when they felt as if they were being lost. They needed a word of providence when they felt alone. But they did not receive this word from the shepherds.

Instead, whenever the shepherds saw the people behaving in a frightened and in a fearful way, they pronounced judgment upon the people and treated them with harshness. They interpreted their sin and guilt as an attempt to run away from God or to be unfaithful to His Law. They interpreted it only that way. They spoke only anger and harshness to the people. They dealt with the sins of the people in such a way that they could interpret the love and grace of God as nonexistent. They pictured a god who is always an angry God, a God of inviolate justice, a God who had no compassion for his people and their sin. Of course, the sheep were driven away by the picture of God as some kind of horrible monster. They were driven away in fear and in fright. They were frightened away because the ministers and the shepherds preached nothing about grace.

This should serve as a reminder for our day and time. If the Word is to be preached in the church, it must be the Word of God's grace and love. It must be the Word which grows out of the covenant relationship which He has created with His people in the Old Testament and in the New Testament in Jesus Christ. If the shepherds would keep driving people away because they have pictured an angry God who cannot forgive, if they would keep driving away the people in their anxiety and in their fears, they are unfaithful to Him who is the Good Shepherd. If a person preaches the Word as only a legal thing, if he preaches only Law, he is driving the people away.

Jehovah Will Restore His Fold

God says He will not permit His people to be continually driven away. He Himself will bring them back. "I Myself will search for My sheep and will seek them out. As a shepherd seeks out his flock when some of his sheep have been scattered abroad, so will I seek out My sheep; and I will rescue them from all places where they have been scattered on a day of clouds and thick darkness. And I will bring them out from the peoples and gather them from the countries. . . . I will seek the lost, and I will bring back the strayed, and I will bind up the crippled, and I will strengthen the weak, and the fat and the strong I will watch over. I will feed them in justice." God will not permit His flock to be ruined by people who dare to ruin it with an unkind word. God will not permit His flock to be ruined by legalism. God will bring His flock back by His own gracious Word. He Himself will seek them out.

Thus we can understand the word which the Lord Jesus speaks in the holy Gospel for today when He says: "I am the Good Shepherd." He is the One who comes to give His life for the sheep. We can understand the word of the apostle in the Epistle for today, who speaks about the Bishop of our souls. The Lord Jesus Christ is the One who bears in His body our own sins, the One who did not revile when He was reviled. He is the One who took upon Himself the burdens of our lives. God performs His act of shepherding in the Lord Jesus Christ. He performs it by the sacrifice which the Lord Jesus Christ made so that we might see God as the Good Shepherd. In the Christ God was searching out His sheep. In the Christ God did come to bring back those who had been the crippled and the hurt by their fears and their anxieties and their sin, their guilt and their shame. In the Christ God does keep this Word, going out to bring back those who had wandered on a dark and cloudy day.

When sheep are frightened, they run, and they run to find their own kind of protection. Stupid little animals that they are, they only get themselves into greater difficulty and hurt themselves more. People do likewise because they have no resources within themselves. There is no self-made way of escape from their guilt and shame, from their fear and anxiety. They try and try all sorts of ways. They try more rebellion. They try to lose themselves in unfaithfulness to wife or children. They try to lose themselves in drink. But they only create a greater problem for themselves. They hurt themselves worse. They destroy themselves.

Though the sheep are driven out on a dark, cloudy day, God is willing to come in the midst of their darkness, in the midst of their blindness, and find them and bring them unto Himself into their land, which is His land. He is their Creator and Father, their Shepherd, who will give them refuge. So if the word of the shepherd is to be preached today, if we are to be the ministers of God, we must minister with His kind of Word. This gracious, healing, saving Word is what we must preach to the people. This is how we must seek them out. This is how we must come to understand their behavior. We must see them in the midst of their behavior as people who are frightened by the world, and we must bring them the Word of grace and reconciliation, which is able to save.

Jehovah Will Feed His Flock

God, who is the Good Shepherd, says that He will not only seek out His sheep but also feed them. "I will feed them with good pasture, and upon the mountain heights of Israel shall be their pasture; there they shall lie down in good grazing land, and on fat pasture they shall feed on the mountains of Israel." God gives His people a diet of goodness and grace. He gives us His Word and holy sacraments. He gives us a steady diet of forgiveness. In the church we are to find a daily forgiveness. It is the church "in which He daily and richly forgives all sins to me and all believers," says Luther. We are to feed on this Word about the good and gracious God, who has given us His love in Jesus Christ. We are to feed daily on the promise that God will never leave us nor forsake us. We are to feed on the promise that God has never given up on us, no matter to what kind of depths of depression and anxiety or sin we have come.

He permits us to be on the mountains of Israel, His holy church, where we are to take this salvation to be ours, and He is the Good Shepherd, who gives His life for the sheep. We are to feed daily on this Word, which says to us that God has prepared for us a new heaven and a new earth. We are to feed on hope and joy. We are to feed on the confidence that no matter how threatening the world may be, no matter how dark the days may appear, He will break through the darkness. He will break through all the threats of the world to give us the confidence that He is the Good Shepherd. This is the kind of Word to which we are to be faithful. A word that would detract from this, that God is the Good Shepherd, is a lie. A word which would detract from this, that God would be faithful to us in His love and grace, is a perversion of the Gospel. A word which would detract from this, that God will continually watch over us, is a detraction from the very Word which God has made good with His own life and death and resurrection.

One can see that this Word is also a word which is going to cut through all kinds of prejudices and biases with which we have been loaded. We are apt to make this Word of God exclusive. We are apt to exclude from this proclamation all kinds of people who desperately need to hear this Word. We are apt to think of ourselves in terms of people who somehow have a corner on the market of God's grace.

The very nature of God's grace demands, compels, and impels us to go out and share this Word with the brokenhearted of the world. We need to share this Word so that people can feed on it in the same way that we are permitted to feed on it.

This is the Word which the prophet speaks to the shepherds of Israel. It is a word which is to remind them that they had been unfaithful to their tasks. And woe to us if we have been unfaithful to that task! Woe to us if we think that somehow we have a special corner on God's grace, that it is intended exclusively for us! The world is crying for this kind of Word, and we need to share it. We need to break out from the kind of provincial attitudes which plague us. We need to live God's grace, live it in such a way that people can tell that we are a part of His flock, that we are a part of His people who taste of His mercies every day, that we are a people who feeds constantly upon the mountains of Israel. Then people may desire to eat of this same goodness each day with us.

The prophet writes that God says: "And I will make them lie down." God will let us have composure and rest. We can stop scrambling all over the world trying to find peace for ourselves. We can stop our scampering and our running to and fro and lie down in peace and know that He is watching over us. That kind of composure comes to dumb, stupid little sheep. The frail little animals have all the forces of the world against them. Yet they lie down in peace and composure and find rest under the protection of the shepherd. You and I in this dangerous age with all the threats of the world hanging over our heads, all kinds of dark clouds and atomic clouds hanging over us, can lie down in peace and composure because God is the Good

Shepherd. He has given His life for the sheep so that we may have life. This we can also share with the world. This kind of composure and confidence is the trust that we can rest secure in the arms of God in this frightening world.

Woe to us if in this day and age we should come and try to frighten the fearful world even more! We should not make the anger of God something great and terrible for the people who are running to and fro, frightened by their own shadows, frightened by the image of themselves. Rather should we picture Him as the Good Shepherd, who is reaching out to gather all the sheep running to and fro, bringing them to His mountain, where they can feed on His grace and lie down in composure. Should we not reach out in this way? Should we not become His faithful shepherds — shepherds who know the Good Shepherd? "For all we like sheep were going astray but are now returned unto the Shepherd and Bishop of our souls." May we then become the instruments of His grace so that even more might be returned to Him.

The Incomparable Holy One

❧ *To whom then will you compare Me that I should be like him? says the Holy One. Lift up your eyes on high and see: who created these? He who brings out their host by number, calling them all by name; by the greatness of His might and because He is strong in power, not one is missing. Why do you say, O Jacob, and speak, O Israel, "My way is hid from the Lord, and my right is disregarded by my God"? Have you not known? Have you not heard? The Lord is the everlasting God, the Creator of the ends of the earth. He does not faint or grow weary, His understanding is unsearchable. He gives power to the faint, and to him who has no might He increases strength. Even youths shall faint and be weary, and young men shall fall exhausted; but they who wait for the Lord shall renew their strength, they shall mount up with wings like eagles, they shall run and not be weary, they shall walk and not faint.* ☙*

Isaiah 40:25-31 (RSV)

❧ *The Incomparable Holy One* ❧

THE confident note of Christ's Easter victory continues to permeate the life of the church through the appointed lessons. Today calls for joy that springs from the resurrection. The church is encouraged to live in this joy in the face of tribulation. The Savior indicates in the holy Gospel that our sufferings and travail are but for a short time and that we shall soon be delivered of them. In the Epistle the apostle reminds us that patience in tribulation is acceptable to God. Our Old Testament lesson is filled with the same kind of note. The lesson is meant as a word of encouragement for the Children of Israel in their Babylonian exile. They are to be encouraged, for in the meanness of their situation the incomparable Holy One remains with them to give them renewal and strength.

Is the Holy One Hiding?

This word was to come with special significance for these people. In the midst of their exile they were likely to feel the loss of their former purpose as the people of God. Their homelessness was not an ordinary displacement. They were uprooted from all the symbols and signs of the homeland that meant they had dwelt in God's promised land. Now they murmured and complained about the severity of their loss. Because they were cut off from the land, they thought themselves cut off from God. The prophet therefore hears of the lament of this people: "My way is hid from the Lord, and my right is disregarded by my God." God apparently had no concern for the exiles. Apparently He did not come to or look over Babylon. Apparently He could not see or He did not care to see the predicament of this people.

Right now in East Germany there must be those who are filled with despair for their situation. In a special edition of the *Sonntagsblatt,* a weekly church paper published by Bishop Hanns Lilje, it was reported that the daily question for the "Church Behind Walls" is: What is God doing? The report comes that the number of those who officially leave the church is small. Those who do leave the church undoubtedly do so because they feel that God is doing nothing in East Germany. They must feel as did the Babylonian exiles: our "way is hid from the Lord." So long as there is no deliverance from the hand of oppression, so long as there appears no escape from the threats to one's liberty to be oneself; so long as it would appear that God Himself refuses to defend His own name, would it not be proper to say, "My way is hid from the Lord"?

We know very well what this means. We ourselves have said it on many an occasion. We have felt it when we have faced difficulties. In our loneliness, our confusion, and the gray darkness of our doubts we have wondered if our way is not hid from the Lord. Where is God to be found when we find ourselves stumbling through our problems? He then appears to be the biggest problem of all. When can He be found if we must be weighted with the millstone of some severe trial? We are apt to think that His absence is the weightiest burden that we have to bear.

Or we are apt to think as did the exiles: "My right is disregarded by my God." What justice could there be for the exiles? Did God behave in a just way if the Babylonians were to live in splendor and prosperity while the people of God should be exiles? Could this be justice if God would give the rule over His people to idol worshipers? Could this be justice that the exiles should lose everything while the Babylonians gained everything? Surely the rights of the children of Judah had been completely disregarded and overlooked. It appeared as if God could not care less. There appeared to be no equity whatsoever in God's dealings with men. He had favored Babylon, but Judah had lost favor with Him completely.

In his essay of 1927, *Why I Am Not a Christian*, Bertrand Russell makes a similar complaint about justice in the earth. Russell mentions that one of the so-called arguments for Christianity is that there must be an ultimate justice. There is so little justice in the earth that one day there will have to be a final reckoning. Mr. Russell retorts that there is so little justice in the earth that there can be absolutely no hope for proper justice at any future date. In other words he is asking the question: If there is no justice now, why should there be justice in the future? Or he might be saying: If God is supposed to rule with justice in the future, why doesn't He do so now?

Does that sound familiar? Doesn't that kind of reasoning go on within our hearts whenever we feel that God has overlooked us? Do we try to rationalize this way when it would appear that God doesn't appear to pay any attention to our rights whatsoever? We feel that there just is no justice at all. We don't appear to have any rights. We seem neglected. What purpose can there be in believing or trying to believe when God does not appear to be interested in our severest and worst problems? No matter in which direction we look, people seem to be having a better time of it than we.

In such moments as these we would sound our groanings with the exiles. God is hidden, or our ways are hidden from Him. There is no justice, or He has completely disregarded our rights.

The Holy One Is Not Hidden

The prophet says no to all of this complaining. God is not hidden. He is very much revealed. All one has to do is look around. God is the One who has created the stars. "Lift up your eyes on high and see: who created these? He who brings out their host by number, calling them all by name; by the greatness of His might and because He is strong in power, not one is missing." The Babyonians may be stargazers and star worshipers, but they do not know the God who has created the stars. Judah should know. Israel should know. God is the God who has created the stars. And He hasn't forgotten them. He still brings them out in their infinite number. When they appear in the heavens, they appear by His beckoning. And He beckons them by name. He sustains and He holds them in their place so that not one of them is missing. So God watches over His people. The God who created the planets, who sustains them, and who governs them in providence is the same God who watches over His people. The people therefore should look up and take heart from this.

Furthermore, "Have you not known? Have you not heard? The Lord is the everlasting God, the Creator of the ends of the earth." The everlasting God, who is transcendent, infinite beyond space and time, beyond finding, is the God who is known and found in the creation, in the ends of the earth. The Infinite One comes to us in the finite. The Everlasting One comes to us in time. The Transcendant One makes Himself known. To Israel this God had come in their history. To us He comes in the Lord Jesus Christ. In Christ we can best understand what the prophet means when He says that the everlasting God is the Creator of the ends of the earth. By this He means to indicate that God accommodates Himself to us in all of the creation. In Christ the whole creation is gathered and finds its meaning and purpose. For in Christ we have the richest proclamation of this God as Creator. In Christ, the Son, the Creature, according to His human nature, we have the best revelation of what God is. Here God is both hidden and revealed the best.

But God is more than revealed in the creation and the creature. "He does not faint or grow weary, His understanding is unsearchable." God does not give up on the world, His creatures, or His people. God had not given up on the exiles. Their ways were not hidden from Him, nor were their rights neglected. God was attentive to them, to their needs, their wants, and their prayers. Their ways had been their own ways and not God's ways. That had been the problem. This was why they were in exile. They had made the exile inevitable because they had failed to trust God. They had made themselves vulnerable by their unfaith. They had brought themselves under subjection. All the while they had been fighting the mercies of God. He had wanted to help them, and they would not let Him. He had wanted to be their God, but they had refused His Word sent by His prophets.

But now their strength had been exhausted. They were held captive. They could fight God no more. They had come to the end of their glory. They would have to rely on His grace. They were broken, and they needed Him to mend them. And this He would do. "He gives power to the faint, and to him who has no might He increases strength. Even youths shall faint and be weary, and young men shall fall exhausted; but they who wait for the Lord shall renew their strength, they shall mount up with wings like eagles, they shall run and not be weary, they shall walk and not faint."

God comes to give strength to all the weak. And all are weak. The youths even grow faint and are weary. None is exempted from needing God as the strength and source of His being. God desires to give His strength to those who are weary and without strength. He would give them renewed life and strength. He would let their spirits soar Godward as on eagles' wings. He would let them run on their own and never get faint. All this means is that God wants us to look to Him from the center of the human predicament of weakness and helplessness. He will be our Help. Instead of bemoaning our helplessness and our inability to find meaning and purpose in it all, we are to look to Him for the strength and the renewal.

We know how He does this in our Lord the Christ. In Christ we come to Him in our utter helplessness, and we see Him who also appeared to be utterly helpless. We see that at the cross. But God raised Him from the dead. He gave Him the renewal. And as the Christ mounted up with wings like eagles at the resurrection, even so will our God give us renewal and strength so that we may run and not be weary; we shall walk and not faint.

Stale Religion

Stupefy yourselves and be in a stupor, blind yourselves and be blind! Be drunk, but not with wine; stagger, but not with strong drink! For the Lord has poured out upon you a spirit of deep sleep and has closed your eyes, the prophets, and covered your heads, the seers. And the vision of all this has become to you like the words of a book that is sealed. When men give it to one who can read, saying, "Read this," he says, "I cannot, for it is sealed." And when they give the book to one who cannot read, saying, "Read this," he says, "I cannot read." And the Lord said: "Because this people draw near with their mouth and honor Me with their lips while their hearts are far from Me and their fear of Me is a commandment of men learned by rote, therefore, behold, I will again do marvelous things with this people, wonderful and marvelous; and the wisdom of their wise men shall perish, and the discernment of their discerning men shall be hid."

Isaiah 29:9-14 (RSV)

◦§ Stale Religion §◦

ONE never has much difficulty in finding someone who would sound off with harsh criticisms of Christianity. This should not surprise us. The church should always be ready to give ear to criticisms that are valid and to defend herself against criticisms that are not. However, the most important kind of criticism which the church must answer is the kind that comes from within. It is the tradition of the church that she must constantly be in a state of reformation. It is presently so. Every major denomination of Christendom is currently engaged in serious soul searching. This is to the good if this theological concern is truly Biblical and properly ecumenical. And we have reason to believe that much of it is.

This is not the first time that the church has questioned herself. We are apt to think of the Reformation of the sixteenth century as a once-for-all reformation of the church. This is a serious mistake. All we need do is take the long look back to see how often God's holy church needed to be reformed to see that we should stand ready to be a part of fresh and new reformations of the church. The prophet serves to remind us of this. The prophet came to speak out against spiritual lethargy and to effect reforms. He was opposed to religion by rote and any religiosity that was stale and indifferent.

Spiritual Stupidity

The prophet was capable of writing with great irony as this piece of Scripture would indicate. The writer was opposed to spiritual stupidity on the part of the people. In an ironic mood he urges the people: "Stupefy yourselves and be in a stupor, blind yourselves and be blind! Be drunk, but not with wine; stagger, but not with strong drink!" The people were not paying heed to his warnings. They gave no heed to his admonitions or to his strong pleas. So He urges them to carry their indifference to its ultimate. They are to behave as stupid people. They are to act as drunken people who have lost their senses. That's what they were. Why not act the part? They were spiritually stupid. They were totally unable to detect when the Word of God made a claim upon them. They were unable to discern that the preachment of the prophet applied to them.

You and I know that there is an enormous amount of spiritual stupidity everywhere about us. But how much spiritual stupidity is there among us? We work ourselves into a state of spiritual stupor when we are unable to relate to the present situation what we confess and believe. Spiritual stupidity has set in when we can no longer read the signs of the times by the aid of the Spirit. Spiritual stupidity grips us when we raise all kinds of religious questions but are indifferent to finding any kind of answers. We cannot escape this criticism of being in a spiritual stupor so long as we are unwilling to face up to the very serious demand which God makes on us by His Word. We cannot escape His demands. Every day He confronts us, and we have to be spiritually stupid to say that He doesn't.

Religious Illiteracy

A second complaint of the prophet is that the people reflected religious illiteracy.

> And the vision of all this has become to you like the words of a book that is sealed. When men give it to one who can read, saying, "Read this," he says, "I cannot, for it is sealed." And when they give the book to one who cannot read, saying, "Read this," he says, "I cannot read."

The prophet reveals the vision that has been given to him. To the prophet it is plain and clear. He declares it in intelligible, clear, meaningful, everyday language. But the intelligent people reply, "We don't get it. It's like a sealed book. The meaning is hidden to us. We can't get at it." And the illiterates say, "We don't get it either. The words are too hard for us."

How many times have you heard that? Or said so yourself? When you come to have the Word explained to you or preached to you or taught to you, this is good. Admittedly the Word is quite often technical. It needs to be explicated. It needs to be studied in concert. We need to speak it to one another, to apply it to one another, to preach it to one another. But how often is it not true that even when we speak it to one another, we say, "We don't get it"! But is it not true that then we do not mean that the language is not clear, the meaning is too difficult, or that it is sealed from us? What we really mean then is that we do not agree with it. We mean that we do not intend to apply this Word to ourselves. We mean then that we will hide behind the excuse that it is too difficult, and we will prefer to be religious illiterates.

Liturgical Lip Service

Another evidence of religious indifference the prophet criticized is liturgical lip service. "This people draw near with their mouth and honor Me with their lips while their hearts are far from Me." Generally the prophets were quite critical of the liturgical services of the people, which became mechanical and beautiful but quite meaningless. The people were able to make their journeys to the centers of worship and to pay their respect and due to God by engaging in the liturgical exercises. They would join in the chants, the psalms, and the prayers with their lips and suppose that they had performed their duty to God. The liturgy became an escape for them. They hid from the real confrontation they should make with their God. They gave their lips to service, but they did not sacrifice their hearts.

Liturgical lip service can be one of our great sins also. The liturgy of the church can be so covered with ritual that one may lose himself in wonder whether he is performing it properly and have no time to surrender his heart to God. On the other hand, the liturgy can become so perfunctory and stale that one could not possibly be stimulated to any real sense of worship. It appears to me that it is this latter which people prefer. They yearn to have the liturgy performed in precisely the same way that they learned it when they were children. They want no variations. They long to sing a few familiar hymns they know by heart. They want no changes. They do not want to learn. They do not want to be led in worship that calls for a commitment of the heart. They want nothing to disturb the comfortable exercise of offering lip service.

Religion by Rote

Another complaint which the prophet levels against the people is that they have a religion learned by rote that supplants the true fear of God. God's complaint is that the people have a fear of Him which "is a commandment of men learned by rote." To memorize the Word of God, to learn it by rote, to be able to recite it is commendable. There is nothing wrong with that. The people were encouraged to commit to memory the Word which God had given. What the prophet complains about is that the people did not use this Word from God. They had learned by rote the commandments of men. Their religion had become man-made. They had developed formulas about God. They had made slogans about God. They had reduced God to words that they could dangle on the string of their memories. They could give recitations about their obligations and duties to God and man. But they did not fear and love God as a personal Being who is involved in all that they did and said.

How easy it is to be identified with that sin! We can quite readily fall back on our catechetical training as a substitute for living in the true fear and love of God. We can make the position of our church body the substitute for giving answer to the questions which God asks of us. We can hide behind the pronouncements of symbols and councils in rattling off answers to questions which the world may ask of us. Now catechetical training and theological formulations are all very necessary, but dare we ever make them the substitute for the proper and true fear and love which we should have for God? We can make theological formulations and pronouncements simply the commandments of men. To do that, each and every one of us has to examine carefully what we believe, to determine that it is not a religion learned by rote that does not call us to stand before our God in fear and love.

God Overcomes Man's Stupidity

How can God overcome all this in His people? What can you do with a people that is bogged down in spiritual stupidity, religious illiteracy, liturgical lip service, and religion by rote? It would appear that God has nothing going for Him. It would appear that whatever God tries is doomed to failure. It would appear that all His efforts come to a sad ending. The prophet thinks not. God will not be frustrated in His desire to win His people. He does not give up with them. He would still win them. "Behold, I will again do marvelous things with this people, wonderful and marvelous." God refuses to turn aside from this people. He had made a covenant with this people. He is bound by the covenant. He will renew His efforts to restore this people as His own. He will do for them what they do not deserve. He will perform His mercy and His grace on them. He will forgive them and take them to Himself again. He will woo them with tenderness. What wonderful and marvelous things will He perform for this people? The following stanzas give a sampling:

"Lebanon shall be turned into a fruitful field." (V. 17)

"The deaf shall hear the words of a book." (V. 18)

"The meek shall obtain fresh joy in the Lord." (V. 19)

"The poor among men shall exult in the Holy One of Israel." (V. 19)

"The ruthless shall come to naught." (V. 20)

"Jacob shall no more be ashamed." (V. 22)

"They shall sanctify My name; they will sanctify the Holy

One of Jacob and will stand in awe of the God of Israel. And those who err in spirit will come to understanding, and those who murmur will accept instruction." (Vv. 23, 24)

In the restoration of this people from the exile in Babylon the people were to know how wonderfully and marvelously God did preserve His people. They were to know some of their former joy, and they were to live in the confidence that God would never forsake His people Israel. They were to know the reality of His dealing in history as a redeeming God. He is truly a God of promise. He performs His wonderful and marvelous acts that His people might know Him as the Holy One, one who is ever gracious toward them.

The fullness of His marvelous action toward His people was to take place in the coming of the Lord Jesus Christ. In Christ God performs all that He said He would do for this people. In the ministry of Jesus we hear over and over again how the deaf hear, the meek are satisfied, the poor are refreshed, and the proud and arrogant are put down. It is the Christ who comes to teach the people with authority and not as their scribes (Matt. 7:29). It is the Christ Himself who applies the prophet's charge of legalism against the pharisees and scribes. (Matt. 15:9)

In the Christ we see how wonderfully and marvelously God deals with us. He draws close to us. He touches us in all our problems. He heals us. He strengthens us. He comforts us. He upholds us. He dies with us and for us. He rises again to give us new life. By so doing He makes good God's pledge to do wonderful and marvelous things for us. He makes clear to us and understandable all that the prophets had announced and proclaimed in the name of God. He reduces to nothingness all the speculation about God. God can be known in this Man. God becomes personal. He is One of us. He is the Holy One among us. He makes it possible for us to love God.

In the Christ we have the means whereby we can shed all spiritual stupidity. God has clearly revealed Himself. His revelation is not difficult. He has opened Himself to us. In the Christ we have the means to overcome religious illiteracy. Christ is not a sealed book. His life is open to us. In the Christ we have the answer to liturgical lip service. He is the Liturgy. His Word is a living, dynamic proclamation of true freedom in which God makes us alive. He comes to us living, alive in the holy sacraments. The sacraments are His action in which He confronts us to claim our hearts. In the Christ we have the answer to religion by rote. As we live each day, we are confronted by situations which we know confronted Him, and someday we face the death He faced for us. But as we face them now, we know we are not alone. He, the risen and living Christ, is with us to assure us that God still does His wonderful and marvelous acts for us.

Prayer with a Purpose

✑ *For thus says the Lord: When seventy years are completed for Babylon, I will visit you, and I will fulfill to you My promise and bring you back to this place. For I know the plans I have for you, says the Lord, plans for welfare and not for evil, to give you a future and a hope. Then you will call upon Me and come to pray to Me, and I will hear you. You will seek Me and find Me; when you seek Me with all your heart, I will be found by you, says the Lord, and I will restore your fortunes and gather you from all the nations and all the places where I have driven you, says the Lord, and I will bring you back to the place from which I sent you into exile.* ✑

Jeremiah 29:10-14 (RSV)

✑§ *Prayer with a Purpose* ξ∾

IN Christendom prayer commands considerable attention. People speak a great deal about prayer because it is a response of the Christian heart to God. Because it is an individual response, people like to talk about the way in which they personally respond to God. But unfortunately too much of the talk about prayer is purely subjective. Consequently we have developed many popular notions about prayer. One notion is that a man may pray in the way in which the spirit happens to move him. Or each can pray in his own particular way. Now this would be true and good if the One who hears prayers would accept the same formula.

However, if we know what pattern of prayer God expects, then the matter becomes different, and we would try to comply with God's views on prayer. This is what the prophet lays before us. He gives us a view of prayer from God's side. It is a view which lays before us the purpose of prayer. It is a view that should enable us to exercise ourselves in prayer with a purpose.

God Sets the Purpose

The first thing the prophet points out is that the purpose of prayer is set by God. It is His purpose that we fulfill in prayer. "Thus says the Lord: When seventy years are completed for Babylon, I will visit you, and I will fulfill to you My promise and bring you back to this place. For

I know the plans I have for you, says the Lord." God has
His will set. He knows what He wants to do. He is not
moved by the whims of man, nor does He move arbitrarily.
He does not give in, does not cater to the petty desires of
people. God has created the creation with a purpose. He
has set His laws in the creation with a purpose. He has
designed His creature man with a purpose, and He desires
that man should fulfill the purposes He has determined.
We cannot expect that by our prayers we are going to alter
or change the mind of God, that we are going to make God
into a different kind of God. That cannot be the purpose of
any prayer. Any such prayer is doomed to failure. It is
not in harmony with the will of God. Any such prayer will
not affect anything or anybody. God's purpose is determined.
His will is set.

But this purpose which God has set is for the welfare of
man. It is a purpose that has promise. "I will fulfill to
you My promise. . . . I know the plans that I have for you,
says the Lord, plans for welfare and not for evil, to give
you a future and a hope." God desires only what is good
for His people. He is a gracious God. And His purpose is
that people should live with blessing and in peace. He does
not intend evil for man. He is not a God who determines
that man should be destroyed but that man should live,
that man should live in Him, that man should live in hope.

God desired this for His people Israel. Unfortunately the
people did not believe that God desired the good for them.
Consequently they went against the will of God. They
fought against God. Instead of achieving their own welfare,
they achieved their own downfall. So God drove His people
into exile. He permitted this for their own good. This had
to happen so that they could understand that they needed

Him and that His purposes were good in the first place. If they had sought Him and trusted Him, they would have lived — lived by His grace and mercy. So God desires that this people should be returned to their former position, that they should live as His people again, that they should know His grace, that they should again be the people of the covenant promise. This is His plan. This is what He has determined for them.

This purpose of God is personal. It is intended for this people, a people that He knows by name, a people that He counts as His dear children, a people that He has watched over and cared for. This is a people into whose history He had entered, a people for whom He had performed a great many wondrous acts so that they could see that He was their personal God, their personal Redeemer and Savior. He had sent them personal words through His prophets. He had performed personal acts for them through His priests. In every way they were to know that this God was effecting His purposes for them. They were to call upon this God in a personal way. They were to seek Him out as a personal Friend and Benefactor. They were to seek Him out as One who would not give up on them, who would always remain dear to them as a Father. He could speak about them as His little children.

We, too, will refer everything to God in the name of Jesus Christ. In the holy Gospel for today we heard how the Lord Jesus speaks to us about asking everything in His name. "Whatever you ask the Father in My name, He will give it to you." And we won't have to ask that Jesus pray for us, He says, but the Father loves us because we have already demonstrated that we love Him through Christ. And so now you are to ask in Jesus' name. Asking in the name of the Lord Jesus Christ of course is not simply a liturgical rubric which we add to all of our prayers by saying that "we ask it in the name of Jesus Christ." Certainly we do that in the world so that people will know that these are Christian prayers. But this is more than a phrase to us. The words mean that when we go to God in prayer, we are going to pray as the Lord Jesus Christ did. To pray in the name of Jesus means to trust as the Lord Jesus Christ did and to plead that God would grant our prayer for Jesus' sake. To pray in the name of Jesus means to confess our total unworthiness of the things for which we pray, asking God to grant them all to us by grace. To pray in the name of Jesus means to live our life as the Lord Jesus Christ did and not need to wonder whether we can ask for this or for that. To pray in the name of Jesus means to make total surrender of our life to God. We will pray in confidence that we are really praying according to God's purposes and that they will be effected.

"You will seek Me and find Me; when you seek Me with all your heart, I will be found by you." We are able to seek God with all our heart through the Lord Jesus Christ. Through Him we determine and know that God is a gracious God. In the Lord Jesus Christ we know that God went to great pains to make it plain to us that He can be trusted. In Christ's death God has reconciled us unto Himself. By Christ's resurrection God assures us that we have new life in Him. God has made it obvious to us through the Lord Jesus Christ that He is a faithful God and that He will not give up on the promises which He has made. He kept His promise to the people of Israel. He did bring them back from Babylon. He did restore His people. He did make them come to the fullness of His promise by sending Jesus

Christ to them. In Christ God revealed His love and demonstrated that He is the gracious God of history that He claims to be.

Thus when we go to our God in prayer, we go in the faith that God will complete the prayer for us, that He will do what we ask of Him because we ask to be heard for Jesus' sake and because by faith in Jesus and by the working of His Holy Spirit we are at one with His mind and will. We have entered into His purpose. This is in effect what we are asking of God in our prayers, that we can become the kind of people that He wants us to be. We ask that we can see His world in the way which He wants us to see. We ask that we can live in history in the way which He wants us to live. We ask that we can discover the kind of purposes that would give us hope and a future. Without this hope we are nothing. Without this kind of view we are simply the old selves that have no future, that have no hope and are inevitably doomed.

From this word of the prophet we can summarize what we need to see in God's purpose in prayer. His purpose is planned. His purpose is intended to work for our welfare. His purpose is personal. When we understand this as we come before God, we may know what is expected of us in our prayers.

Prayer Is a Surrender to God's Purpose

Our prayers are to be an act of surrender to God. We are to give up on ourselves. This is to say that we are no longer to live by our own purposes, by our own notions of things and our own view of things. We are not to live in the world as if we could determine how the world should be operating and how we ourselves are to act in the world. Rather in our prayers we are to seek out the purposes of

God by surrendering to His will. We are not to act contrary to God. We are not to ask Him to change His view of our situation. Rather we are to change our view of the situation with Him in it. So we find God's purpose by surrendering ourselves. This is what God says: "Then you will call upon Me and come and pray to Me, and I will hear you. You will seek Me and find Me; when you seek Me with all your heart, I will be found by you."

When we are ready to give up our hearts in a total act of surrender and faith to God, not only will we seek to find His purpose, but we will also then refer everything to God. We will permit Him to be God, permit Him to rule in our lives. We will permit Him to rule in the earth, and we will acquiesce to His rule. Then we shall see that the way He performs things in the earth is the best way for us. We shall see that the way in which He acts toward us through the ministration of the sacraments and the preaching of the Word is what is best for us. We shall acquiesce to God because we shall see Him acting and moving in the earth for the welfare of mankind.

This will mean that many times the world will seem upside down to us. It will appear to us that what men determine to be the good is just the opposite of what God determines as good. This is very often the case. We shall see that the human view of things is rarely the divine view of things. We shall see that very often men have to suffer in order to accomplish God's purposes. We shall see very often that men will have to be hurt by the world if they are to do that which is pleasant and good before God. Yet we shall be ready to surrender and give ourselves to the hands of God because we know that everything has to be referred back to Him who is the Lord of creation and history. There is no other way. Our prayers will be acts in which our minds will search what His will is and in which we shall refer everything to Him to perform for us.

In our prayers we then discover that we are one with all the family of heaven. We discover that we have a power and strength which we did not have before. In our prayers we discover a righteousness and a joy which we did not have before.

It is a painful process to come to this kind of position in prayer. It is painful to have to give up on yourself and your own notions. It is painful to give up on the idea that we can push God around and dictate to Him what He should do. It is painful to give up on the idea that we are able to make God do our bidding. But it is a great experience to know that God has changed us. It is a joy to know that He has given to our lives a dimension that was not there before. And the more we understand the responsibility of this kind of prayer, the more we understand the responsibility of prayer with a purpose. Sometimes we may find it difficult to pray thus, to face up to the things that God asks of us. Yet once we have prayed thus, once we know in our hearts that God can make a great change in us and that He can perform His acts in us, then we shall find that such prayer becomes easier and easier. We shall also find the kind of joy and the kind of hope that God promises to us. So that would be the effect of our prayer.

Prayer with a purpose is prayer with a purpose set by God. It is His purpose accomplished in us. Prayer changes not so much things but people. God changes us by our prayers.

We offer ourselves in prayer, yet it is God who is offering Himself. We gain a victory in prayer, yet it is God who gains the victory. We surrender ourselves, yet it is God who has surrendered Himself. We pray that His will be done, and His will is done in us by our prayer.

He does all this in our prayers that we might have a future and a hope.

The Promise of the Spirit

⋘ For the palace will be forsaken, the populous city deserted; the hill and the watchtower will become dens forever, a joy of wild asses, a pasture of flocks, until the Spirit is poured upon us from on high, and the wilderness becomes a fruitful field, and the fruitful field is deemed a forest. Then justice will dwell in the wilderness, and righteousness abide in the fruitful field. And the effect of righteousness will be peace, and the result of righteousness, quietness and trust forever. My people will abide in a peaceful habitation, in secure dwellings, and in quiet resting places. And the forest will utterly go down, and the city will be utterly laid low. Happy are you who sow beside all waters, who let the feet of the ox and the ass range free. ⋙

Isaiah 32:14-20 (RSV)

The Promise of the Spirit

TODAY in the holy Gospel we hear our Lord give promise that He would send the Comforter, the Holy Spirit, to His disciples. This lesson is intended to prepare us for the Feast of Pentecost. We are reminded of the manner in which the church awaited the glorious fulfillment of this promise. But what happens to you and to me as we await the fulfillment of the same promise in our lives? Are we to await some radical change? Is something new to appear on the scene? Are we suddenly to be changed? Are we to have new feelings? What happens when God does give His Spirit to man?

Various answers have been given to these questions. There are those who insist that some kind of inner adjustment must take place if man is to possess the Spirit of God. Or they would suggest that the possession of the Spirit is a strengthening of man's attempt to find his way to God. Or to put it another way, to have the Spirit is to be lifted up in the search for God. Such attitudes have been the most prevalent in the life of the church. They are responsible for creating doubts in the hearts of many as they wonder whether they have the Spirit of God. Or these attitudes also delude people into believing that their simple piety is an assurance that they have the Spirit of God.

The Old Testament prophets had a different concept of

238

the promise of the Spirit. For them the coming of the Spirit is an act of God in which He lays hold of man and performs in him what He will.

Life Without the Spirit Is Desolation

To understand this, we must first understand what life without the Spirit is. Life without the coming of the Spirit is desolate. It is incomplete. It lacks its proper purpose. It can never come to fulfillment. Instead, life without the Spirit continually empties itself. It is drained of whatever resources it may claim for itself. Its hopes, its dreams, its goals are regularly dashed and ruined until it is finally crushed by death itself.

This is what the prophet foresees for any and all who are in any way complacent about life. In the preceding verses of this stanza he scolds the women of Jerusalem for the gay manner in which they danced at the festival of harvest. Apparently they gave every indication that the warnings of the prophet had no effect on them. Now he issues them an invitation to dance their dances at the festival of their destruction in a little more than a year from the date of their festival celebration. Then everything will be destroyed. Their complacency will be shattered. The harvest will fail. Their homes will be overrun with bramble and briers. The palace will be deserted, the city empty. Because these people did not see that they had forsaken God, God would furnish them with the dramatic evidence that they had. They would see life devoid of all blessing. They would experience how far-reaching, how all-encompassing their desolation without the Spirit is. In the midst of their emptiness they would recognize their desolation.

Those of you who have read or have seen performances of Samuel Beckett's drama *Waiting for Godot* will remember how this modern playwright has characterized the various attempts to solve the human dilemma. The characters in the play are acting in a vast wasteland that appears to grow larger and more foreboding as the characters fail to give purpose to their existence. The play heightens the desolation of man without purpose. Just so the prophet here intends to make his point for the women of Jerusalem. Not as though man somehow could afford the luxury of living without the Spirit of God. Life without the Spirit of God is the ruination of life. It spoils all of life. It ruins the very creation itself. What the women of Jerusalem are now celebrating will soon be the cause for their lament. The very creation is scorched by their sin. It dries up in the same way that their faith has withered.

Thus we should always find life without the Spirit of God. Eventually we should feel this emptiness in all life. For the moment we may be able to fill ourselves with something else. We may preoccupy ourselves with the festival dances before our favorite idols — reason, pleasure, wealth, or self. But sooner or later we should have to join in the dirges at the death of these gods. And quite often the day of mourning comes sooner than expected. When the idols we create collapse and fail us, then we know what this desolation is whereof the prophet speaks. We sense this desolation in every fiber of our beings. We may feel lost or lonely, depressed or anxious, worried or fearful. In those moments the whole creation appears to be threatening, our friends appear to be unsympathetic or unable to understand. We feel alone and cut off. It is then that we know how deeply we are affected by the lack of the Spirit. Our feelings are not simply a disorientation of the emotions, but our whole person seems stretched and racked with the pains of futility.

And should we cling to the idols through all of life, then in our death we should come to utter desolation.

The Life of the Spirit Is Life

However, the coming of the Spirit to man is the enrichment of all of life. When the Holy Spirit comes to man, God changes His whole situation. The prophet pictures this coming of the Spirit as the dawning of a new age. He contrasts this to the desolation which the people of Jerusalem would experience. They would experience this desolation because they were already desolate. But after they recognize their utter desolation, then God would pour out His Spirit from on high. Then a new day would dawn for His people. "The wilderness becomes a fruitful field, and the fruitful field is deemed a forest. Then justice will dwell in the wilderness, and righteousness abide in the fruitful field. And the effect of righteousness will be peace, and the result of righteousness, quietness and trust forever. My people will abide in a peaceful habitation, in secure dwellings, and in quiet resting places."

Certainly such a life is what men long for. Men have lived, worked, and died in the attempt to make such a picture of life a reality, and yet they appear to be frustrated in their efforts. However, the New Testament church, the church of Pentecost, believed that this day has dawned. In Peter's sermon on that day in Jerusalem he proclaimed that God had poured out His Spirit from on high. The many utterances of the prophets concerning the coming of this day were regarded as completed and fulfilled on that day. The faithful in Jerusalem regarded themselves under the power of the Spirit. They believed that they had been acted upon by God Himself. They felt a part of the new age, the new era in which they could recognize God's creative hand. They believed they could live in justice, righteousness, peace, quietness, and trust.

The way by which they came to this conclusion must be viewed from the events of the life, death, resurrection and ascension of our Lord the Christ. They had followed Jesus because they believed Him to be the Messiah. They many times displayed their ignorance of what He was to do as the Messiah, yet they persisted in their faith in Him as Messiah. When His death approached, they displayed the greatest ignorance concerning His work. Even after His resurrection they were ignorant of what His death and resurrection meant. But prior to His death He had given promise of the coming of the Spirit. The Spirit would teach them all things and bring to remembrance everything that Christ had taught them (John 14:25, 26). And the Holy Spirit would testify concerning the Christ and bear witness to Jesus (John 15:26). Now they knew. Pentecost was the dawn of a new era. It was the dawning of faith in Jesus as Christ and Lord. It was an awakening to the fact that Jesus was Christ and Lord in His death, resurrection, and ascension. To have the Spirit of Christ is to know Jesus as Christ and Lord.

Thus it is that when we recognize this Christ as the Christ for us, we, too, enter into the new age. The work of the Spirit is God's work upon us. It is God coming to us. This is not some kind of indefinable essence which we suddenly possess within ourselves. It is not some new quality which we take to ourselves. The coming of the Spirit is God's act in which He seizes us in the midst of our sin and our desolations and draws us up into the life of Christ. The coming of the Spirit is God's act in which He comes to us in the midst of our emptiness and fills us with the love of

Christ. The coming of the Spirit is God's act in which He comes to us in the midst of our guilt and gives us the righteousness of the Christ. The coming of the Spirit is God's act in which He comes to us in the midst of our fear of death and gives us the hope of the resurrection in Christ.

Regin Prenter in a study of Luther's concept of the Spirit shows how Luther viewed the Holy Spirit as *Spiritus Creator,* the Creator Spirit. The same Spirit who created the heavens and the earth out of nothing comes to re-create us out of nothing. When by our confession we come to understand that we are nothing before Him, that we are desolate and empty without Him, then He descends upon us with His love and re-creates us by making us conform to the death and resurrection of Christ. In Baptism and daily confession He makes us conform to the death of Christ and raises us to new life. In the Lord's Supper He feeds and nourishes us with the righteousness of Christ. In the Word He bestows this Christ upon us.

In the coming of the Spirit God takes over our lives in Christ Jesus. The whole life, our creatureliness, our mind, our reason, and our senses come under the rule of God. We step into the new age. The Christ becomes a present reality for us, for in Him we learn to know God as the gracious God who acts for us to create new life out of our daily dying to sin in confession. The life of the Spirit, or after the Spirit, then is not some psychological shifting, but it is the totally new life which we are able to live by faith in this Christ. It is in Him that we find justice and peace, righteousness, and trust in the wilderness of the wastelands of this tired and dying world.

The Outpouring of the Spirit

&⸲ *And it shall come to pass afterward that I will pour out My Spirit on all flesh; your sons and your daughters shall prophesy, your old men shall dream dreams, and your young men shall see visions. Even upon the menservants and maidservants in those days I will pour out My Spirit. And I will give portents in the heavens and on the earth, blood and fire and columns of smoke. The sun shall be turned to darkness and the moon to blood before the great and terrible day of the Lord comes. And it shall come to pass that all who call upon the name of the Lord shall be delivered; for in Mount Zion and in Jerusalem there shall be those who escape, as the Lord has said, and among the survivors shall be those whom the Lord calls.* ⸲&

Joel 2:28-32 (RSV)

⇜ *The Outpouring of the Spirit* ⇝

PROBABLY to most people the outstanding feature of the first Christian Pentecost is the large number of people who confessed Christ that day. Many would still put a great deal of stock in the kind of numbers that a modern-day revival or Pentecostal meeting might attract. The crusades and the rallies are counted successful to the degree that they fill the stadia or convention halls and list a large number of conversions.

That kind of emphasis is totally lacking in the New Testament. The first large numbers of people that were added to the church at Jerusalem were from the ranks of the chosen people. The effect of those first sermons by Peter was to identify for the people the One for whom they waited. Peter demonstrated how Jesus had fulfilled the covenant and that by the resurrection and ascension God had exalted Jesus to be the Christ.

This is the emphasis of Pentecost. The numbers are incidental here to show that God had kept His promise to the house of Israel and that He had renewed His Zion. From this point on, from Jerusalem outward, the preachers of the covenant fulfilled were to spread their message with amazing zeal, but they were also to find stiff resistance in many quarters. Little evidence is given of the numbers of people that the church won, but there is a wealth of material to show that God continued His activity of the outpouring of the Spirit. The matter of what God does in the giving of His Spirit is what should occupy our hearts and minds today.

The Spirit Creates Faith

When Peter preached on Pentecost, he quoted from the Book of Joel the words of this text. He indicated that the words were fulfilled in what was happening in the Holy City that day. The people of Israel for a long time had longed for the fulfilling of these words of the prophet. Hope had settled on this people as they anticipated with eagerness the dawning of the day when they could know that God's Spirit had been poured out upon them. The prophets had been quiet for many years. No new word appeared on the scene to give them the indication that the day had come. Many words there were, but they were always new words of speculation about how and when the new era of the Spirit would come.

What had happened this day that Peter could say in confidence that this was the day of the coming of the Spirit? For one, Peter could declare that the faithful had been given the gift of discernment. They could compare spiritual things with spiritual (1 Cor. 2:13). They could understand what had been hidden to them before (John 16: 12-14). They could speak with authority (1 Peter 4:11). They could speak boldly (Acts 4:20). These were clearly new abilities. These were proficiencies which formerly had belonged to those rare and chosen men, the prophets. These were the gifts of the men who had had dreams which they interpreted as messages of God. These were the skills of the visionaries who spoke of the visions which God gave to them. Peter identified himself and the faithful as the prophets, the dreamers, and the visionaries of whom Joel wrote.

The vision and the dream, the prophetic Word of which Peter spoke that day, had to do with the Christ. The faithful had seen heaven opened in the risen Christ. They had seen the dream of God become a reality in the perfect mission which Jesus accomplished in the name of God. The prophetic Word had been spoken in the Christ. The realization of these dreams and visions made the faithful at Jerusalem confident that the Holy Spirit was working His holy work upon them.

So God continues to work His precious work in our hearts. The word of the prophet is fulfilled in our lives when we have confidence and trust in the Christ who died and rose again for us. This is the blessing of the prophet, of the holy dreamer and sanctified visionary. When they can identify God's love, His grace, His forgiveness as God's action for them in Jesus of Nazareth, they have the gift of the Spirit. To know that God is ever gracious toward us, just as He has revealed in Jesus Christ, is to have the specialized gift of the Spirit. To know that God will remain faithful in His love toward us in spite of our sin is to have the Spirit of the visionary. To know that God acts decisively for us in the Word and the sacraments is to have the Spirit of the holy dreamer. To know that our most heinous sin is to fail to trust God's compassion and mercy is to have the Spirit of the prophet.

The Spirit Is Available to All

The amazing feature of this outpouring of the Holy Spirit is that it is available to all His people. The prophet indicates that God intends to pour out His Spirit upon all flesh, upon the sons and daughters of Israel, upon old and young men, even upon the menservants and maidservants.

This almost seemed to be an impossibility, that God would provide this rich gift to all His people, that He would perform this upon ordinary people. The Lord Jesus had promised this gift to the disciples, and now on the Pentecost Day the disciples stand as evidence that God fulfilled this promise. You will recall that Peter's sermon on Pentecost Day was an answer to the accusation of the people that these men are filled with new wine. Peter says: "No! We are not filled with new wine. We are filled with the Holy Spirit. Remember the Word of the prophet. Remember the word of the prophet Joel that people would be able to prophesy and dream dreams and have visions. This is being fulfilled in us now. We know what God did in Jesus Christ. We know what God accomplished in our hearts through all that is said by the prophets and now is fulfilled in Jesus."

Peter was saying: "Here we stand, ordinary, uncultured, unlettered people. You don't believe that this could be a possibility for us, but God has made it possible. We would never have imagined that we would be able to be prophets. We would never have realized that we would have visions and have dreams, were it not for the fact that we stand here now able to speak to you, able to speak to you with conviction, able to discern what God has accomplished, and able to make a witness to what God has done in Jesus Christ. This is because God has poured out His Spirit upon us."

Then Peter went on with that sermon to say: "For the promise is to you and to your children" (Acts 2:39). In essence he was saying: "It is promised to you and to your children. You can have the very same gift which we have who are standing here among you and speaking to you about these things of God. It is for you. It is available to all people. It is available to every man who would understand, believe, and trust what God has done in Jesus Christ." That was a remarkable notion which Peter introduced, and yet it was not new. It certainly was not new to what the prophets had been saying before him. It was not new to what God had performed for His people in the Old Testament. It is in harmony with what God is doing in Christ for His people all along. It is what God wants to do among us here now. God would pour His Spirit out upon us in the same manner that He did upon the faithful on that first Pentecost Day. He says the same words to us. He gives us the same kind of promise, and He gives us the same degree of the Spirit. If we would only trust Him, He would perform this among us. God desires to draw us up into His life the same way in which He drew the great saints of old. God desires to impart His Spirit upon us in the same measure as He did for these people.

Somewhere Luther says "If I had enough of the Holy Spirit, I could write Scripture." His point is this, that we are not to think of the Holy Spirit as being held back from us somehow, that God in some way is trying to hold back a little bit so that we will not enjoy the same kind of grace, the same kind of love, the same kind of mercy as did these people here on that first Pentecost Day. No, God would pour this out richly upon us so that we could, if we believed enough, go on to perform these great works in His name. And the fact is that we can. We can trust, we can rely on God's mercy, we can hold Him to His promises the same way in which the early church did. God is just as faithful today as He was then.

The Outpouring of the Spirit

The Spirit Employs Signs

The third feature of the first Pentecost Day, also one which we would like to see repeated, is the kind of signs which were promised by the prophet Joel and to which Peter referred. "I will give portents in the heavens and on the earth, blood and fire and columns of smoke. The sun shall be turned to darkness and the moon to blood before the great and terrible day of the Lord comes. And it shall come to pass that all who call upon the name of the Lord shall be delivered; for in Mount Zion and in Jerusalem there shall be those who escape, as the Lord has said, and among the survivors shall be those whom the Lord calls." You remember that on Pentecost Day the record indicates there appeared to the disciples "tongues as of fire" (Acts 2:3), and that there was "a sound from heaven like the rush of a mighty wind" (Acts 2:2). You will recall, too, from the accounts of the resurrection of our Lord that the earth trembled and quaked. You will remember also that when Jesus died on the cross, there were great signs in the earth. All these things are mentioned in the Gospels to give an indication that God was acting in the creation in accordance with what had been predicted by His prophets. The whole earth quakes and trembles as God performs His mighty acts upon men. And as God performed His work of outpouring the Holy Spirit upon the disciples, there again were signs. Signs of the creation, as of fire and the sound of a wind, were indications that God was stirring the creation as He stirred the hearts of men.

What are the signs today? we are going to ask. The very people to whom Peter preached asked the same thing: "What shall we do to be saved? What are we going to do so that we can have the same kind of experience that you

251

have had? What are we going to do so that we can know
that we are affected by the Holy Spirit? What are we going
to do so that we can be absolutely sure that God has touched
us, that He has set us on fire, that He has given us His
Spirit?" Peter says: "Repent and be baptized, every one
of you, in the name of Jesus Christ for the forgiveness of
your sins; and you shall receive the gift of the Holy Spirit"
(Acts 2:38). This is the sign. This is God's use of the creation. To give you an indication, or sign, that God has poured
His Spirit upon you, He pours His water upon you. Here is
the sign of the creation for you, that you know that you as
a creature are caught up into God's new creation. Here is
proof for you that the old creation is washed away, that
you are a part of the new. You can know and be assured
that God is ever faithful toward you.

So today we are to remember the sign that God has performed upon us. As certainly as He covered the disciples
that day with a sign as of fire, so He has covered our heads
with His holy righteousness in Holy Baptism. Today also,
as we come to the Sacrament of the Altar, we are reminded
again that here are signs of the creation. Here is bread and
wine that He takes and uses to give us Christ's body and
blood and at the same time His righteousness and His holiness. As certainly as the bread and wine become a part of
you, so certainly His righteousness becomes a part of you.
Here are signs that the promise: "Your sons and your daughters shall prophesy, your old men shall dream dreams, and
your young men shall see visions," applies also to us today.
We are not kept apart, we are not kept out of the realm of
God's holiness; God pours out His Spirit richly upon us. We
can be assured that as we go forth this Pentecost Day, we
can go forth with the gift of God's Spirit.